COLLECTOR'S COMPASS™

20ᵗʰ Century Glass

Martingale
& C O M P A N Y

Bothell, Washington

Credits

President . . . . Nancy J. Martin
CEO . . . . Daniel J. Martin
Publisher . . . . Jane Hamada
Editorial Director . . . . Mary V. Green
Editorial Project Manager. . . . . Tina Cook
Series Editor . . . . Christopher J. Kuppig
Design and Production Manager . . . . .Stan Green
Designer . . . . .Bonnie Mather
Series Concept . . . . Michael O. Campbell

Collector's Compass™: 20th Century Glass
© 2000 by Martingale & Company

Martingale & Company
PO Box 118
Bothell, WA 98041-0118 USA
www.martingale-pub.com

Printed in Canada
05 04 03 02 01 00   6 5 4 3 2 1

   The information in this book is presented in good faith, and while every precau-
tion has been taken in the preparation of this book, the publisher assumes no responsi-
bility for errors or omissions. The publisher disclaims any liability in connection with the
use of this information. For additional information please contact Martingale &
Company, PO Box 118, Bothell, WA, 98041-0118.

Library of Congress Cataloging-in-Publication Data
Collector's Compass: 20th century glass
     p. cm. — (Collector's compass)
   ISBN 1-56477-344-2
      1. Glassware—Collectors and collecting. 2. Glassware—History—20th century.
      I.Title: Twentieth century glass. II. Series

NK5110.A15 2000
748.2'075—dc21   00-042369

Mission Statement
We are dedicated to providing quality products and service by working
together to inspire creativity and to enrich the lives we touch.

TM

CONTENTS

FOREWORD

As America's favorite hobby, collecting is exciting, gratifying, and above all, fun—but without the right knowledge, you could be destined for disappointment. Luckily, you've just found the most resourceful and inspiring series of guidebooks available to help you learn more about collecting. The Collector's Compass series approaches collecting in a whole new way, making it easy to learn about your favorite collectible categories—from the basics to the best-kept secrets.

The International Society of Appraisers (ISA) is pleased to be associated with the Collector's Compass series. As the ISA celebrates 20 years of professional education and certification of personal property appraisers, who currently specialize in over 200 areas of expertise, we remain committed to setting the highest standards for our accredited members. The Collector's Compass series of reference books reflects the ISA's dedication to quality and integrity.

Christian Coleman, ISA CAPP, Ret.
Executive Director, International Society of Appraisers

INTRODUCTION

Whether it means setting the alarm clock for Saturday morning yard sales, watching "Antiques Roadshow," or chasing down childhood memories on eBay, collecting has become America's favorite hobby. The joy of finding treasure amid the clutter of a tag sale or a screen full of online offerings is infectious. Who could resist a pastime that combines the fun of shopping, the thrill of the hunt, the lure of a bargain, and the pride of ownership?

Throngs of novice collectors are joining experienced veterans in online bidding and weekend "antiquing" expeditions. If you count yourself among them, this book is for you.

The editors of Collector's Compass realized that today's collectors needed more information than what was available, in an accessible and convenient format. Going beyond available price and identification guides, Collector's Compass books introduce the history behind a particular collectible, the fascinating aspects that make it special, and exclusive tips on where and how to search for exciting pieces.

Furthermore, the Collector's Compass series is uniquely reliable. Each volume is created by a carefully chosen team of dealers, appraisers, and other experts. Their collaboration ensures that each title will contain accurate and current information, as well as the secrets they've learned in a lifetime of collecting.

We hope that in the Collector's Compass series we have addressed every area essential to building a collection. Whether you're a newcomer or an experienced collector, we're sure this series will lead you to new treasures. Enjoy the adventure!

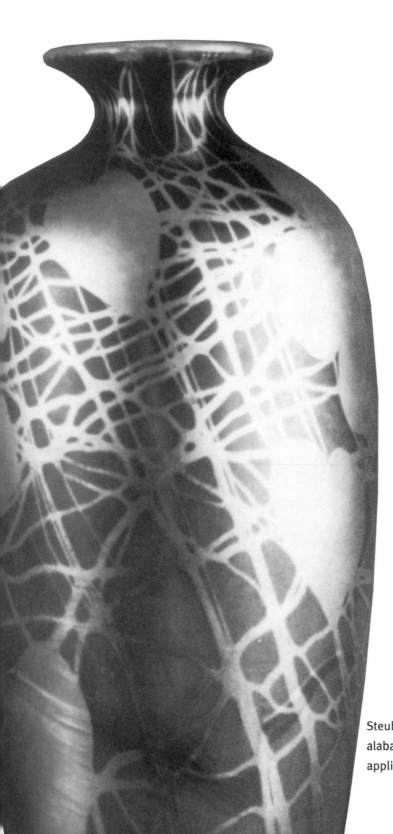

Steuben vase, gold ruby over
alabaster with gold aurene
applied design, c. 1910

GLASS AS A COLLECTIBLE

Glass collecting is a hobby enjoyed by thousands of people, young and old. While the popularity of individual types of glass waxes and wanes, glass collecting has endured as a timeless pursuit over many hundreds—even thousands—of years.

With its rainbow of glittering colors, glass has been blown, cut, etched, engraved, pressed, molded, gilded, enameled, spangled, spattered, stretched, threaded, twisted, and ruffled into every conceivable functional and decorative form. No wonder, then, that it is a perennial favorite, constantly attracting new collectors.

The Special Allure of Collecting Glass

People love to collect glass for reasons as diverse as the colors and styles in which it may be found. The primary reason most collectors cite is "Because it's beautiful!"

Collectors love the shaded colors of art glass, such as Amberina made by the New England Glass Company, the Mt. Washington Company, and Hobbs, Brockunier in the late 1880s. Or they admire the beautiful enameling of birds, animals, and portraits on Crown Milano.

Tiffany, Steuben, and Loetz collectors like iridescent colors in gold, blue, and even rainbow patterns. French cameo glass collectors find beauty in naturalism and difficult cameo techniques.

Lalique collectors admire stylized designs, opalescent colors, and stained effects.

People are often drawn to elegant or pattern glass originally used in fine table settings as a touchstone of American manners and traditions of times past. Many collectors buy pieces to add to a tableware pattern used by their mother, grandmother, or other family member. Women, especially, remember glass used on festive family occasions in childhood and now wish to set their own tables with the same pattern.

Men, on the other hand, are often drawn to glass collecting because of the fascinating techniques and fine workmanship it displays. These collectors can spend many happy hours examining a single piece of cameo glass, trying to determine whether it was acid cut, carved, marvered in, padded or stained, or crafted with a combination of these techniques.

And, while those who own rare Lalique or Tiffany pieces worth many thousands of dollars are content to display them safely out of harm's way, the vast majority of glass collectors *use* their glassware. To be used is, after all, the purpose for which most of it was intended. Elegant glass —stemware and a myriad of specialty serving dishes —evokes an earlier time when everyday etiquette called for the elaborate table settings that we reserve for only the most special occasions and holidays today. Thus, our love for fine collectible glassware adds tremendous nostalgic context to our entertaining and family gatherings.

Indeed, reasons for collecting are as limitless as possibilities for glass collections. Perhaps your interest in glass is newfound, or you

> ### Born to Be a Collector
> A teenager living in Long Island in the late 1940s started collecting Tiffany during a period when nobody wanted it. The prices were cheap, and he thought the glass very beautiful, even though he had no formal knowledge of the history of Louis Comfort Tiffany and his body of work from the 1890s to the 1930s. This boy, now in his sixties, still loves Tiffany glass and has a magnificent collection.

Tiffany favrile centerpiece, 1900–1920s. *Courtesy of Collector's Showcase.*

want to add to a cherished collection inherited from your great-grandmother. Or maybe you've admired the glass collections of others and want to start one of your own but haven't yet settled on a niche. Whatever the case, this book will help you explore ways to plan and build your collection. Then it will guide you through the marketplace, helping you find the best shopping venues and warning you about pitfalls and common errors.

Glass Types and Categories

This book concentrates on the most-collected areas, or categories, of fine glass made in the past one hundred and twenty years. A clean demarcation at the beginning of the twentieth century is artificial, because many of the most significant glass makers had begun production in the latter half of the nineteenth century, and their wares evolved organically—favorite styles and patterns staying on for decades, while less successful lines were discontinued—right into the new century. Thus, our focus is on what you're likely to find in the marketplace—represented in the various venues we will discuss. This scope of coverage spans the late-Victorian period to the late-twentieth century. Here are some descriptions and definitions of the categories discussed throughout the book (and a brief mention of some categories that aren't).

Art Glass

Fine ornamental glass made after 1885 in the United States, England, France, Bohemia, Italy, Scandinavia, and other European countries is generally considered *collectible art glass*. Obviously, there are some people who collect older glass, but it is more expensive and much scarcer, so this book will concentrate on the glass that is still widely available.

Tiffany candy dish, signed. *Courtesy of Collector's Showcase.*

The style of art glass made at the beginning of this period is called *Late Victorian* or *fancy glass*. Made in England and the United States as well as Bohemia, this glass is characterized by lots of color, with shading from red to amber or salmon to pale yellow (and, more rarely, other color combinations). It was decorated extravagantly: enameled; layered in various ways, such as with mother-of-pearl air trap patterns; cut back, as in the English cameo; or filled with mercury. It was adorned with flowers, gilded, and spangled. Stylistic influences were the colorful and fluid shapes of Venetian glass and the simple forms and subtle colors of Chinese glass, with a little Japanese naturalism thrown in.

Art Nouveau period glass followed, circa 1900. French *cameo glass* was made in colors of jade and other semiprecious stones. The motifs of Emile Gallé, probably the single most important artist of the period, were inspired by the naturalism and asymmetry of Japanese prints and native French plants and flowers.

Other Art Nouveau artists, including René Lalique, were influenced by the flowing reverse-curve design often referred to as the *whiplash.* Their designs incorporated beautiful young maidens with long, flowing tresses, often drawn from famous actresses of the day, such as Sarah Bernhardt and Loie Fuller.

In the United States, Louis Comfort Tiffany and his workers experimented with spraying metallic vapors and oxides onto the surface of still-hot glass, barely etching it but causing the surface to refract the light, creating a lovely iridescent effect of many hues. He called his glass *Favrile,* meaning handmade. He subsequently utilized Favrile glass in a variety of applications that included vases, stemware, tableware, and his famous lampshades.

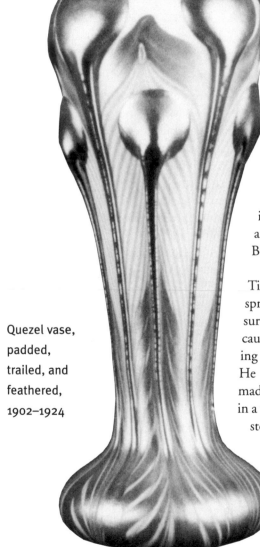

Quezel vase, padded, trailed, and feathered, 1902–1924

Tiffany's work gave rise to many competitors, Frederick Carder of Steuben being the most important. Carder made a glass similar to Favrile called Aurene. Durand, Quezel, Nash, even Union Glass of Somerville, all made art glass. Handel & Company made Art Nouveau lamps, but in styles dissimilar to Tiffany's.

Dozens of French companies did important work. Among the most-collected are pieces made by the Daum Brothers, who are still in business, Muller Frères, and G. Argy Rousseau. In Austria, Loetz-Witwe was the leading company in innovative designs.

In the 1920s the preferred style changed from Art Nouveau to *Art Deco* (Décoratif). It was characterized by symmetry, strong geometric or repeating patterns, black outlines, and primary colors. Lalique's strongly stylistic molded glass became the icon of the period. There were many imitators of Lalique both in France and the United States, including Verlys, Sabino, Etling, and Hunebelle.

There were numerous Art Deco glass companies in Europe. Some of those in France were Schneider, Delatte, and Daum. Baccarat, a French glassworks dating from the early eighteenth century started producing Art Deco-style tableware and commercial perfume bottles.

A new kind of art glass called *graal* glass was developed at the Orrefors Glassworks in Sweden in 1916. It was similar in technique to French cameo glass, but had an outer layer of clear glass.

Orrefors graal dish, 4¼" diameter, by Edward Hald, signed "Orrefors S. Graal 1806L Edward Hald," 1954

The clear glass Orrefors used for engraved pieces became the prototype for the clear modern glass produced by Steuben since 1933, and by modern Daum, Baccarat, and St. Louis in France. Many companies, including Kosta and other companies in Sweden, Iittala and others in Finland, the Hadeland Company in Norway, Holmegaard in Denmark, Val St. Lambert in Belgium, and Royal Leerdam in Holland, emulated the new Orrefors glass.

Yet another important development was made in Murano, Italy, by Paolo Venini in the 1920s. The new styling of Venini glass had elements of Art Deco styling. It was geometric in form and pattern, but had the brilliant colors and furnace techniques of the master blowers of the old Murano families. This led to a whole new era of modern glassmaking in Murano and Venice, where the craft has been practiced since the thirteenth century.

Studio Glass

In 1962, two Americans, Harvey Littleton and Domenic Labino, conducted a workshop for studio glassmakers. Littleton had designed a small furnace that made it possible to fire glass in small studios, as an alternative to factory furnaces.

This invention led to new glass schools and a worldwide movement that continues today. It is known as the studio glass movement, and its product is called simply *studio glass*. Many artists produce one-of-a-kind pieces, but others do small-scale production work or limited series. The innovative glass made by these studio artists is among the best glasswork ever done by anyone, anywhere, and some of it is undercollected. This book will make recommendations for collecting affordable studio work.

Dale Chihuly, an American, has become the best known of the studio artists, and his work commands very high prices. He creates the designs and directs a small team of glassworkers who execute the pieces.

Elegant Glass

High-quality, mass-produced tableware and stemware made by numerous U.S. glass companies is called *elegant glass*. It is characterized by fine glass of excellent clarity with high polish.

Everything from complete sets of dinnerware and stemware to decorative accent pieces was produced in crystal and colored glass. Elegant glass may be plain or etched, cut, enameled, overlaid, or reticulated.

Most of the companies that made elegant glass began in the 1900s, producing Early American pattern glass and utilitarian wares. Beginning in the early 1920s, these companies—Heisey, Cambridge, Fostoria, Imperial, Duncan-Miller, and many others—produced tons of elegant glass, well into the 1950s. Elegant glass of the 1920s and 1930s was thinner, more decorative, and more colorful than that produced in the late 1940s and early 1950s.

Early American Pattern Glass

The terms *pattern glass* and *pressed glass* mean the same thing: clear or colored glass molded into a predetermined pattern. An astonishing number of patterns were made by hundreds of companies such as Heisey, Cambridge, Greentown, Imperial, U.S. Glass, Fostoria, and National.

Early American pressed glass, *flint,* first produced about 1825, was made with a leaded formula and produced a ringing sound. Lead became scarce during the Civil War, and in 1864 the company Hobbs, Brockunier developed a soda lime formula to replace it. Glass-pressing machines improved during the same era, and mass production of quality tableware ensembles began in earnest. Many companies produced scores of matched place settings and serving pieces in each pattern.

Depression Glass

Made from circa 1920 to 1940, *Depression glass* was basically an inexpensive machine-made pressed glass that reproduced or mimicked pattern glass. It was sold at popular prices, and is generally collected by pattern and color.

Depression glass was made by Jeannette, Anchor Hocking, Hazel Atlas, Federal, Indiana, and Imperial, among many others. It was often given away as a special premium, especially by theaters, or packaged with other products as a promotional item.

Other Glass Collectibles

There are a number of types of glass that are avidly collected but not covered in this book:

Cut glass ginger jar, 1920s. *Courtesy of Collector's Showcase.*

- *Kitchenware:* Utilitarian tableware, bakeware, juice reamers, refrigerator storage ware, and jars for canning
- *Advertising glass:* Molded and screen-printed glasses, jars, and canisters used as original packaging or created for promotional purposes, such as Swanky Swigs (cheese glasses) and Coca-Cola bottles as well as other soda fountain glass
- *Bottles and flasks:* Pharmaceutical and commercial bottles, and molded glass flasks
- *Barware:* Shot glasses, shooters, beer mugs, ashtrays, and the like
- *Commemorative ware and souvenirs:* Glass objects such as toothpick holders, ashtrays, plates, mugs, and goblets; often made to mark historic events, political campaigns, wars, or as exposition souvenirs
- *Industrial glass:* Optical and laboratory glass as well as glass insulators used on telegraph, telephone, and electric power lines

---

Always Use Two Hands

One collector of art glass recalls her beloved mentor, who taught classes in glass identification and history. The teacher's home was a living museum, and her students sat at her dining room table surrounded by cabinets of rare glass. She allowed the students to handle, examine, and admire her wonderful *objéts d' art.*

The first lesson she taught was how to hold fine glass. "Always use two hands. Hold it on the bottom and move slowly. Never pick up pieces by the handle or by applied parts."

Where Can You Find Collectible Glass?

Glass satisfies the "collecting bug" because of the great range of types, colors, and shapes to be found, its wide availability, and the range of prices. There is a glass collection out there waiting for any budget. You can often add a wonderful serving piece to your favorite setting of pattern glass for twenty or thirty dollars. Depression and Carnival glass occasionally may be had for even less. But if your taste runs to original examples of fine art glass by the best artists, you'll have to spend several thousand dollars to add to your collection.

The easiest places to find glass are specialized glass shows, general antiques shows, antiques shops, special glass auctions, Internet auction sites such as eBay, as well as Web sites devoted to glass.

For the well-informed and tenacious, glass of all kinds still may be found in thrift shops, flea markets, and at garage and yard sales. There are so many deliberate fakes and copies, as well as authorized (but still confusing) reproductions, that it is risky to buy from anyone other than a dealer who will give you a written guarantee.

Estate sales are often a source of great finds, but be prepared to hunt down a *lot* of these sales before you find anything. And be aware that prices are sometimes higher at estate sales than at antiques shows!

Most experts advise novice collectors to attend several glass and antiques shows before buying. Carefully examining and handling all that glass is a wonderful eye-opener. When you know you're holding "the real thing," often you can learn to judge authenticity by weight, balance, and "feel."

Dealers at these shows are often knowledgeable about glass and happy to share information with collectors. Another

Quezel "Jack in the Pulpit" vase, a lovely example of Art Nouveau design

Crossover Collectibles

It's fairly common for people to start by collecting art pottery and then cross over into art glass. Other collectors concentrate on all kinds of Victoriana, or collect Art Nouveau furniture, silver, and jewelry, as well as art glass. Object collectors who may, for instance, collect inkwells or paperweights, are likely to include glass examples along with silver, bronze, and porcelain in their collections.

advantage of shows is that you don't have to make a decision as quickly as at an auction. And you can bargain with most dealers over price.

And now the Internet! There are new Web sites every day, and eBay auctions are boundless. The downside of buying on the Internet is that you can't handle and examine the glass, which is very important. There is stiff competition for prized pieces; instead of bidding against three collectors at a local auction house, you could be bidding against dozens all over the world.

"Before You Start Collecting" (page 43) will explore each of these secondary market venues in detail and will provide the tools to help you collect confidently and wisely wherever you shop.

Planning Your Collection

Experts say it is always advisable to start a collection with a narrow focus. This is important for a variety of reasons:

- With so many types of glass available, it's easy to simply get "lost." Without a focus, many beginners get distracted, buy "mistakes" that they soon come to despise, and become overwhelmed or discouraged that their collection isn't "coming together."
- You'll be in competition with sophisticated collectors. You need to do in-depth research on your chosen specialty *before you buy anything.*
- Unless you have unlimited means—and not many of us do— your money is best spent amassing a clearly defined collection focused on quality and depth. You can always branch out into other areas later, as your tastes and interests change.
- Some popular ways to organize collections are discussed below, but you may discover that coming up with your own original scheme is as much fun as buying a special treasure.

Pattern

Most, but not all, collectors of pattern glass collect all the pieces of a given pattern they can find. The goal is to have a complete set or, occasionally, sets of a pattern in each color produced. Some collectors search for a single example of every pattern they like, or every pattern made by one company.

There are a few collectors who want a distinctive pattern of art glass, such as the King Tut pattern of Durand. Lalique collectors are also anxious to collect certain designs. All Lalique designs have names, and the same designs or patterns were executed on different forms, some in different colors.

Type of Ware

A common organizing principle is to collect, say, candlesticks and candelabra in many patterns and colors, or sugars and creamers in sets. Vases and goblets are especially appealing to many collectors. One collector specializes in one-of-a-kind goblets and uses them only for special occasions. They reside on custom shelving around the top of her den so the family can enjoy the various shapes and colors daily, between those rare times when they are brought down.

Artist or Designer

Art glass collectors often specialize, buying only Tiffany pieces or the colored Steuben designed by Frederick Carder. Other workmen and designers are also identifiable, and some people look for the work of a particular one. Emil Larson designed for Durand and Dorflinger (among other companies), and there are collectors who look for his glass, signed or unsigned, with the help of books documenting his work.

Durand "King Tut" vase, 1920s

Color

Some collectors care only about color. They want their glass to be cobalt blue or cranberry, and little else matters. Others want to find at least one item in every color ever produced.

17

> **'Tis the Season**
> An innovative family of collectors has amassed so much glass that the family members have made holiday decor a tradition. They've installed custom shelving in several rooms and display their red and green glass at Christmas, red and crystal for St. Valentine's, and green for St. Patrick's day. They even have an amber and black display for Halloween!

Manufacturer

Collectors sometimes look for pieces from only one company, or may collect any and all American-made glass.

Theme

Some people choose a common theme for a collection, such as a variety of glass animals or only Cambridge swans. One eclectic collection we've seen features hand-painted Fostoria vases, Sabino figurines, and glass butterflies. Above all, collect what you like, what gives you joy.

Series

One collector has all the Carnival glass Christmas plates that Fenton Glass Company produced in the 1970s. Other collectors look for similar series made sporadically by several U.S. glassmakers.

Remember, no two collectors (or their collections) are the same. Individuals may look for perfection in color, technique, and complexity, as well as the right signatures and provenance (history of ownership). Some want only rare or unusual pieces. Some will buy only signed pieces—a good rule for beginning art glass collectors.

A display of Fostoria hand-painted vases; Cambridge geisha glass lamp at upper right

The Best Resources for a Glass Education

Read all the books you can find in your chosen area of glass. Attend glass shows, and handle and examine all the glass you possibly can. Join a collector's club—better yet, join several. And visit the museums with specialized glass collections so you know what the finest examples in mint condition look like.

Read and Research

In "Essential Background for Glass Collectors" (page 23), we survey some of the important glass designers and companies. We suggest further reading for each and note relevant clubs and museum collections. The recommended books will lead you to others, and soon you'll be able to hold your own in the marketplace. *Glass Collector's Digest* is a worthwhile bimonthly magazine devoted solely to collectible glass.

Trade papers and club newsletters are essential reading, as well, if you want to keep up with current glass trends. They often carry classified advertisements, important for researching prices and helping to locate glass you're seeking.

Join a Club

Other collectors are the best possible source of information, and the programs and seminars conducted by many of the clubs are an irreplaceable part of your glass education.

There are national clubs with local chapters, and dozens of additional clubs that specialize in the preservation of one manufacturer or one type of glass. Through the books, newsletters, catalog reprints, and lectures produced by these associations, a permanent document is available to today's collectors, as well as generations of the future. Some collecting societies even maintain their own museums and libraries.

Virtually every club publishes its own newsletter, and some produce books. Most newsletters apprise members of glass shows, auctions, exhibits, programs, lectures, and other events of interest. Many include directories of shops, collectibles auctions, and other related events and services. Some clubs periodically produce limited-edition pieces for their memberships' exclusive purchase, usually from original molds that have been preserved by the club.

During the summer months, many collecting societies hold conventions with shows, seminars, programs, and special events that make the trip worthwhile. A visit to a convention is another great learning experience and provides an opportunity to make friends with collectors from all over the country.

The National American Glass Club is an "umbrella" organization with many chapters around the country. Members collect and study about all periods of glass, all types of glass, and glass from all over the world. The members include many glass curators from museums, as well as collectors. *The Glass Club Bulletin,* which is published quarterly, contains articles about glass and a calendar of events. The club sponsors an annual seminar in a different U.S. or Canadian city.

Individual chapters of The National American Glass Club hold monthly meetings to view glass collections and to study and present various glass topics. Some individual chapters organize glass shows; otherwise, there is no selling through the club.

There are other clubs and associations for more specific interests. There are clubs for collectors of perfume bottles, paperweights, Carnival glass, Depression Glass, Heisey glass, Duncan Miller glass, cut glass, and the list goes on. See "Resources to Further Your Collecting" for a listing with addresses and other contact information.

Imperial Elephant, from an old Heisey mold. Imperial produced this piece in numerous transparent and slag colors. *Photo courtesy of the Heisey Glass Museum.*

Museums

Museums with glass collections are a superb resource for experienced as well as novice collectors. Every would-be collector should visit the Corning Museum of Glass. Nowhere else will you see such splendid examples of virtually every type of glass ever produced. Corning has the world's premier exhibit of glass antiquities, going back thirty-five hundred years, but it doesn't give short shrift to modern glass. Other excellent glass exhibits are listed in "Essential Background for Glass Collectors" (page 23) with their respective areas of specialization.

Don't forget the museums founded by specialized glass clubs, such as Heisey and Cambridge. It's invaluable to see these collections, even if you actually buy another kind of glass. See "Resources to Further Your Collecting" for listings with contact information (page 125).

Value and Price Trends

A perennial collectible, glass generally maintains fairly stable values, although prices for some types are more volatile. Overall values of American-made elegant glassware have increased 20 to 30 percent over the last five years. In many cases, values have doubled in the past ten years.

During the 1980s and early 1990s, glass collecting enjoyed a heyday. It was extremely popular, and many new collector clubs and organizations were founded. As we start a new millennium, the market for glassware has leveled off, with prices softening in some areas. Other collectibles, such as American art pottery, are claiming the interest of many collectors.

However, some categories of glass are extremely "hot." When someone publishes a new book on one manufacturer or type of glass, with a price guide included, examples of that particular glass-ware escalate in price almost overnight. During the initial period of heightened attention resulting from the book's publication, some pieces sell for extremely overvalued prices. But, since astute collectors know that the market won't sustain these prices, demand declines and some dealers are stuck with inventory for which they probably paid too much. Collectors may never get their money out of pieces they've purchased.

One area in which prices have hit bottom is defective and damaged glass, almost no matter what a piece's attribution or how rare it might be. Collectors have become more sophisticated as more books are published and as they are increasingly able to net-work with other collectors through clubs and the Internet. Years ago, even savvy collectors might buy defective glass to fill a "gap." No longer.

The market for American-made Victorian art glass has been fairly stagnant for some years, although it has picked up a little

COLLECTOR'S COMPASS ™

Never set out to collect solely as an investment—it's an enterprise doomed to failure. Yes, a small fraction of collectors make a fortune when they sell, but the odds are no better than in playing the lottery. *Collect what you like,* learn everything there is to know about it, buy the highest quality pieces you possibly can, and the likelihood is that your collection will appreciate steadily.

recently. It was wildly popular until the 1970s, when Art Deco took off. Art Nouveau has remained strong all along.

Tiffany glass prices have been high for a long time and may always be prohibitively expensive. Tiffany is a risky area for new buyers, even if they are affluent. Tiffany lamps, Favrile glass, and Tiffany signatures have been faked for years and are still being faked.

Since Victorian art glass prices have not risen as much as Art Nouveau prices, very fine examples are still comparatively inexpensive. Regional price differences are often evident: Victorian art glass will sell for less in New York City than it will in Cleveland or other Midwest cities. Art Nouveau glass will be lower in the South than in Chicago.

Thoughtful, well-defined art glass collections are likely to increase in value during the next ten years because more people will be trying to find less and less glass. The museums have acquired a great deal of the very best glass and will continue to do so as pieces come on the market. And because glass is fragile, breakage will lessen the supply even more, so prices will go up.

Studio glass will likely continue to command high and escalating prices, in secondary markets as well as in galleries.

ESSENTIAL BACKGROUND FOR GLASS COLLECTORS

Glassmaking traditions are rich and dramatic. Virtually every culture in the past five thousand years has contributed new materials, techniques, and designs. No wonder, then, that glass is collected almost universally for its beauty, its documentation of artistic efforts, and its usefulness.

American glass production began in the New England states and gradually moved south to New York and New Jersey, then west to Pennsylvania, Ohio, and West Virginia. You'd visit the latter states today to tour working factories. These manufacturers followed abundant water, sand, and fossil fuel supplies.

One of the things most fascinating—and exasperating!—about glass companies is the amazing degree to which they were bought, sold, and merged. If you're a fan of detective novels, you might enjoy following the clues to sort out mysteries surrounding your glass specialty. One company, A.J. Beatty & Sons, merged with U.S. Glass in 1892 and became known as Factory R. But collectors refer to its wares as "Tiffin glass" because it was produced in Tiffin, Ohio, even though that was never the company name. To further thicken the plot, the merged company later merged with Duncan-Miller Glass Company and made Duncan-Miller pieces in "Tiffin" colors!

*Learn More About the
History of Glass*

Read:

American Glass,
George S. McKearin and Helen
McKearin

Glass, 5000 Years, Hugh Tait,
ed.

Nineteenth Century Glass,
Albert Christian Revi

Join:
The National American
Glass Club

Visit:
Corning Museum of Glass

Carnegie Institute Museum
of Art

Museum of American Glass at
Wheaton Village

National Museum of American
History, Smithsonian
Institution

Most of the American glass production in the 1800s was utilitarian, although decorative lines were made. It was not until well into the twentieth century that the elegant glass so popular among collectors showed up en masse in factory showrooms.

Glass sales were declining in the later teens, so companies needed to introduce new products. In the early 1920s, showrooms were ablaze with pink, green, blue, yellow, black, orchid, and amber dinnerware and decorative items. This love affair with color continued until the outbreak of World War II, when raw materials necessary for color production were designated for military use. Manufacturers reverted to crystal production, but now they etched, carved, and enameled their wares. After the war, color production exploded again, but the colors were even more vivid: favorites in the 1940s and 1950s were cobalt blue, ruby, and emerald. These brilliant tones continue to attract avid collectors.

This section provides an overview of late nineteenth and all of twentieth-century glassmaking by looking briefly at a few of the hundreds of artisans and companies in the United States and Europe that did—and, in some cases, continue to do—important work. Remember, this is only the tip of the iceberg—a way of introducing you to the glassmaking tradition and perhaps helping you narrow your collecting choices. Some key references, significant collections, and collector's clubs are mentioned for each glass producer, so it's easy to find out more about these—and other—glassmakers. (Addresses, bibliographic data, and contact details are provided in "Resources to Further Your Collecting.") Use this as your stepping-off point for further research into the area that interests you.

Brilliant Cut Glass

This type of clear glass was made by a number of American companies between the late nineteenth century and the 1950s. First popularized in America at the Centennial Exposition in 1876 and the Columbian Exposition of 1893, brilliant cut glass was made by grinding intricate, light-reflecting patterns into blown glass blanks using an abrasive wheel, and then painstakingly polishing each cut. Many of the manufacturers did not sign their wares before 1890. Companies such as Libbey and Hawkes used acid-etched marks thereafter, but major brilliant cut glass works such as Dorflinger, Corning, and Meridan rarely, if ever, signed their work. Brilliant cut glass ranged from petite toothpick holders to massive punch bowls, compotes, and lamps.

Hobbs, Brockunier & Company

A company renowned for its brilliant cut glass was Hobbs, Brockunier of Wheeling, West Virginia. William Leighton, in charge of production, devised a soda lime formula that revolutionized the industry by making a less expensive, crystal clear glassware.

The company's most spectacular art glass was named Coral but is now known only as "Wheeling Peach Blow." It has shades from red to yellow and is lined in white. Both matte and shiny versions were made. It was introduced by Leighton and sold from 1886–1891, when Hobbs was bought by the U.S. Glass Company.

Learn More About Brilliant Cut Glass

Read:

Dorflinger: America's Finest Glass, 1852–1921, John Q. Feller

American Cut and Engraved Glass, A. Christian Revi

Join:
American Cut Glass Association

Visit:
Corning Museum of Glass

High Museum of Art

Learn More About Hobbs, Brockunier

Read:

Hobbs, Brockunier & Co. Glass, Tom Bredehoft and Neila M. Bredehoft

American Glass, 1760–1930: Toledo Museum of Art, vols. 1 & 2, Kenneth Wilson

From the New England Glass Company to Libbey-Owens

The New England Glass Company of East Cambridge, Mass-achusetts, was renowned for its shaded art glass. Glass artist Joseph Locke developed the technique, in which part of the glass was reheated in the furnace, in the 1880s.

opposite: New England Glass Company plated Amberina, 1886

Among the types of distinctive shaded glass most popular with collectors:

• Transparent Amberina, shading from red to amber, first made in 1882
• Plated Amberina, first made in 1886, opaque lined
• New England Peach Blow, shading from dark pink to white, opaque and not lined; made from 1886–1890
• Agata, made by coating Peach Blow with metallic stain, spattering the surface with alcohol, then firing; invented in 1887

The shapes of some of the opaque items are similar to Chinese pottery forms. None of this glass was signed.

In 1890, New England Glass, owned by the Libbey family, was moved to Toledo, Ohio, reorganized, and renamed. Most Libbey Glass Company production in the first half of the century was brilliant cut glass, but various kinds of art glass were made until around World War II. Libbey glass was signed with its name after 1890. Today, the company is the industrial giant Libbey-Owens.

Learn More About New England Glass and Libbey
Read:

Libbey Glass since 1818: Pictorial History and Collector's Guide, Carl Fauster

Nineteenth Century Glass, Albert Christian Revi

Mt. Washington Glass Company

Mt. Washington, of New Bedford, Massachusetts, came out with a version of Amberina soon after the New England Glass Company. It created a different Peach Blow coloration, now very rare, with shading from pale mauve pink to pale blue. Burmese, an art glass with shading from salmon to citron yellow, was Mt. Washington's first distinctively different color formula. Burmese was also made, under license from Mt. Washington, by Thomas Webb & Sons in England. Webb's wares have come to be known as "Queen's Burmese," after Queen Victoria. They were often decorated with enameled flowers or animals, and the shapes are different from those made by Mt. Washington. None of them was signed.

Crown Milano, an opaque, satin-finish, single-layer decorated fancy glass, was often signed "CM" or, rarely, "Albertine." This glass premiered in 1886, although it was not patented until later. In 1894, Mt. Washington patented Royal Flemish, a frosted transparent glass that was decorated to look like sections of stained glass windows. It was a single-layer glass, adorned with stained and gilded subjects such as Guba ducks, Roman coins, angels, or heraldic animals. This glass is sometimes signed "RF" on the bottom.

Throughout its history, Mt. Washington made pressed, blown, lava, cameo, cut, Napoli, and Verona glass, both before and after it merged with the Pairpoint Manufacturing Company, a New Bedford silver-plating firm, in 1894.

Learn More About Mt. Washington and Pairpoint
Read:
Pairpoint Glass, Leonard E. Padgett

American Glass, 1760–1930: Toledo Museum of Art,
vols. 1 & 2, Kenneth Wilson

Join:
Mt. Washington Art Glass Society

Visit:
Chrysler Museum of Art
Jones Museum of Ceramics and Glass

Thomas Webb & Sons/Stevens & Williams

In the Stourbridge area of England, there were two companies that specialized in art glass during the late 1880s and continuing into the twentieth century. During the fancy glass period, Thomas Webb & Sons and Stevens & Williams were both influenced by Venetian glass with its bright colors, applied flowers, and small handles. Both companies also produced work influenced by Chinese pottery, mimicking the simple shapes and matte colors, *casing* the glass to get opaque effects.

The cameo glass made by Webb and Stevens & Williams (and others) was inspired by cameo glass from the ancient Roman period.

Learn More About English Glassmakers

Read:

English Cameo Glass in the Corning Museum of Glass,
  Dr. David Whitehouse

Carved & Decorated European Glass,
  Ray Grover and Lee Grover

English Cameo Glass, Lee Grover and Ray Grover

British Glass, 1800–1914, Charles Hajdamach

Whitefriars Glass, Leslie Jackson, ed.

Emile Gallé

The towering genius in glassmaking, Emile Gallé of France, set the standards for what eventually became known as Art Nouveau glass. He studied botany and Japanese prints in the 1870s and, by the late 1880s, created a new type of cameo glass. He combined two or more layers of glass and then cut it back to reveal designs influenced by naturalism and asymmetry.

He died in 1904, and his company continued until 1932 under other management. In order to see fine examples of Gallé glass, go to the Corning Museum or to the museum in Nancy, France, Gallé's hometown. Rare pieces of Gallé art glass are occasionally sold at one of the major auction houses, usually for tens of thousands of dollars.

Gallé glass is always signed, but now there are a great many fake pieces and fake signatures. It is extremely risky to buy Gallé glass except from a totally reliable source that provides documentation.

Daum Brothers

There were many imitators of Gallé. The Daum Brothers, also of Nancy, France, were the first to start working in his Art Nouveau style. They did high-quality cameo glass, eventually branching out with designs that showed their own originality.

The Daums are particularly noted for their *paté de verre*—a molded, powdered glass, or glass paste—especially the outstanding work done by Almeric Walters, an artist who worked for Daum.

Daum remains one of France's premier art glass producers, still admired for its modern paté de verre artists and designs.

René Lalique

René Lalique began his artistic career designing Art Nouveau–style jewelry.

When he turned to glasswork, commercial perfume bottles became an early specialty. In about 1910, he began the glass company dynasty that continues today with his granddaughter, Marie-Claude Lalique. During the 1920s and 1930s, he designed many series of molded glass. Some is frosted, some tinted, some colored. The original designs are very high style Art Deco motifs. He, too, was influenced by Emile Gallé's emphasis on nature. Many of Lalique's designs were of birds and fish. He also used figural motifs.

The work of René Lalique's son, Marc, done after 1945, as well as that of his granddaughter are very good and certainly collectible. However, designs done by family members haven't achieved the importance to collectors—or the prices—of René Lalique's glass.

> ### *Learn More About Gallé, Daum, and Lalique*
> **Read:**
> *The Art of Glass: Art Nouveau to Art Deco*, Victor Arwas
>
> *The Art of French Glass*, Janine Bloch-Dermant
>
> *The Art of René Lalique*, Patricia Bayer and Mark Waller
>
> *Lalique Glass*, Nicholas Dawes
>
> *The Art of Emile Gallé*, Phillipe Garner
>
> *Daum. Masters of French Decorative Glass*, Clotilde Dacri
>
> **Join:**
> Lalique Collectors Society
>
> **Visit:**
> Corning Museum of Glass
>
> The Toledo Museum of Art
>
> Metropolitan Museum of Art

Fostoria Glass Company

Exceptionally fine tableware and stemware were the hallmarks of Fostoria Glass Company. Founded in Fostoria, Ohio, in 1887, the factory moved to Moundsville, West Virginia, in 1891 and stayed in production there until 1986, when the plant closed.

Many Fostoria patterns and colors were specifically designed to compete head-to-head with Cambridge and Heisey. The company's wildly popular American pattern was made in a wide array of pieces. Many of its other patterns are quite collectible, including Camelia, Coin, Fairfax, June, Kashmir, Navarre, and Versailles.

Fostoria water goblet with blue stem, 1920–1930s.
Courtesy of Star Center Mall.

Learn More About Fostoria
Read:

Fostoria Glassware, 1887–1982, Frances Bones

Fostoria Stemware: The Crystal for America, Milbra Long and Emily Seate

Fostoria Tableware, 1924–1943, Milbra Long and Emily Seate

Fostoria Tableware, 1944–1986, Milbra Long and Emily Seate

Fostoria Useful and Ornamental: The Crystal for America, Milbra Long and Emily Seate

Join:
Fostoria Glass Association

Fostoria Glass Collectors

Fostoria Glass Society of America

Visit:
Fostoria Glass Society of America Museum

Huntington Galleries

Louis Comfort
Tiffany vase

Learn More About Tiffany

Read:

Louis Comfort Tiffany, Alastair Duncan

Louis C. Tiffany: Rebel in Glass, Robert Koch

Art Glass Nouveau, Ray Grover

American Art Nouveau Glass, Albert Christian Revi

Tiffany Favrile Art Glass, Moise Steeg

Visit:

Chrysler Museum of Art

Toledo Museum of Art

Corning Museum of Glass

Historical Glass Museum Foundation

William Benton Museum of Art (University of Connecticut)

Tiffany Studios

The most well-known and influential American art glass company of the twentieth century was Tiffany Studios. Louis Comfort Tiffany, independently wealthy, established a company in 1893 in Corona, New York. He was not a glass blower or decorator, but a designer who directed a team of workers.

Tiffany designed stained glass windows for churches and private homes. His secular work was distinguished by beautiful florals and landscapes, as well as by the fact that he used glass alone, in various colors and textures, to create his designs. Other artists typically used painting to create fine detail in stained glass work.

When he began designing leaded glass lamps, he established another company, Tiffany Furnaces, to make the metal bases for his lamps as well as other metalwork.

Tiffany's Favrile blown glass became emblematic of what was later called the American Art

Nouveau style. Actually, much of his work was inspired by Roman glass, rather than French Art Nouveau. While Tiffany is best known for his use of gold and blue iridescence, he created other kinds of glass, including *lava, agate reactive, paperweight, aquamarine,* and many others.

A.H. Heisey Glass Company

Noted for the clarity of its glass and its popular patterns, Heisey began production in Newark, Ohio, in 1896. Favorite patterns include Empress Blank, Lariat, Orchid Etching, Pleat and Panel, and Yeoman.

The company produced a great deal of blown, as well as molded, glass. Its custard glass is among the most coveted collectibles. Also favorites among collectors are the Heisey pieces that combine cutting, etching, and silver deposit, as well as the figurines produced from the 1930s until the factory closed in 1957.

Heisey marked its work with a distinctive stylized H inside a diamond. However, Imperial bought many Heisey molds when the factory closed and reissued patterns, some in colors that Heisey never used.

> ### *Learn More About Heisey*
> **Read:**
> *Collector's Encyclopedia of Heisey Glass, 1925–1938,* Neila Bredehoft
>
> *Elegant Glassware of the Depression Era,* 8th ed., Gene Florence
>
> **Join:**
> Heisey Collectors of America
>
> National Capital Heisey Collectors
>
> **Visit:**
> National Heisey Glass Museum

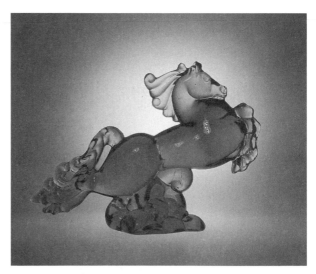

Imperial Flying Mare from a Heisey mold, 8⅞" high, 1982. *Photo courtesy of the National Heisey Glass Museum.*

Scandinavian Glass

Scandinavia has a tradition of innovative glassmaking. Two of the better-known companies are Orrefors and Kosta.

Orrefors Glassworks

Located in Smaland, Sweden, Orrefors Glassworks was begun in 1898. At first it made only simple jars, table glass, perfume vials, and the like. Then, in 1910, the glassworks was bought by Johan Ekman, an aristocratic Swede who wanted the production to become more artistic and modern.

Ekman hired Simon Gate, a Swedish painter trained in the classical style of art. Gate trained with master glassblower Knut Bergqvist and the two developed a new technique called *graal* (grail): layers of colored glass were cut back into a pattern, and then covered with another clear layer of glass to make a smooth surface. In 1917, Orrefors hired Edward Hald, who worked there until 1978. He and Gate became the company's superstar designers.

Orrefors won every top prize in European expositions throughout the 1920s and 1930s and pioneered the designer-and-worker system that was adopted by all the Scandinavian glassworks. The pure, clear, modeled glass of Orrefors inspired the clear Steuben glass of the 1930s, as well as glass made by modern Daum. Orrefors continues to be a commercial and artistic leader. It makes fine tableware, art glass pieces, and unique sculptures.

Orrefors fish-graal, designed by Edward Hald. Between 1936 and 1982, 23,000 pieces of this design were made, each different.

Kosta

The oldest Swedish glass company still in existence, Kosta followed Orrefors' example in the twentieth century. In 1948, Kosta hired designer Vicke Lindstrand, who had worked for Orrefors for ten years.

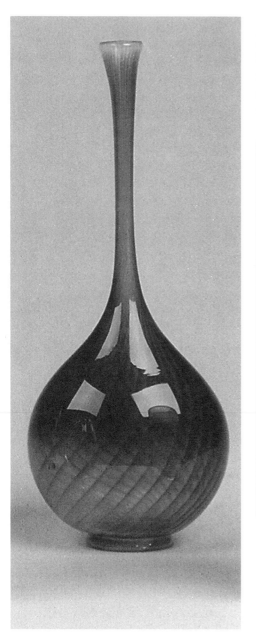

Another glassmaking genius, Lindstrand was the Kosta artistic director from 1950 until 1983. He designed in every imaginable technique: blown, engraved, cut, cameo, graal, and some special methods he invented.

Learn More About Scandinavian Glass

Read:
Scandinavia: Ceramics and Glass in the Twentieth Century, Jennifer Opie

Swedish Glass Factories Production Catalogues, 1915–1960, Helmut Ricke and Lars Thor. ed.

Orrefors, a Century of Swedish Glassmaking, Kerstin Wickman, ed.

Visit:
Corning Museum of Glass

Smålands Museum, Småland, Sweden

Glasmuseum, Ebeltoft, Denmark

Finnisches Glasmuseum, Riihimäki, Finland

Kosta "Colora" vase designed by Vicke Lindstrand, 13" high.
Photo courtesy of Wright.

Bohemian Art Glass

The province of Bohemia is one of the historic glassmaking areas of Europe. A brief discussion of three important factories will give you a little background.

Loetz

The company commonly called Loetz was known in the late 1800s and early 1900s for making Art Nouveau glass somewhat similar to Tiffany's iridescent glass. For many years, unsigned Loetz glass was often misidentified in auctions as "Tiffany." Now the production has been thoroughly researched. Loetz used different shapes and different types of iridescence. *Papillon* (butterfly wing) iridescence was unique to Loetz.

Some of Loetz's talented glass artists were commissioned to make glass for the *Wiener Werkstatte* (the Vienna Workshops) in the early 1900s. The early Vienna Workshop style was geometric in form, simple, using a lot of innovative cutting, enameling, and other techniques. It still has an impact on contemporary design.

Loetz went bankrupt in 1932. It was bought and owned by several Germans during World War II. In 1945, the Czech government nationalized the company and then closed it.

Moser

The Ludwig Moser & Söhne Company, of Karlsbad, is known for its extravagant late-nineteenth-century colored and enameled glass. This company also executed designs of the Vienna Workshop, as well as those of the Vienna Secession. The Vienna Secession was a group of renegade Viennese artists who, in 1903, held a show that initiated a style inspired by the designs of Charles Rennie Mackintosh of Glasgow, Scotland, in its geometric and elongated forms. The elegant Vienna retail glass shops Lobmeyr and Bakalowits commissioned Moser, as well as Loetz and Meyers Neffe, to produce art glass in the Vienna Secession styles.

Piece attributed to F. Schmoranz, probably commissioned by Lobmeyr, executed by the Meyers Neffe factory in Bohemia, c. 1890

Learn More About Bohemian Glass
Read:
The Art of Glass: Art Nouveau to Art Deco, Victor Arwas

Glas Verre Vetri, Waltraud Neuwirth

Bohemian Glass, 1400–1989, Sylva Petrova and Jean-Luc Olivie, eds.

Bohemian Glass, 1880-1940, vols. 1 & 2, Deborah Truitt and Robert Truitt

The Moser Company went bankrupt in 1932. The banks ran it until 1939. After World War II, in 1945, Moser was nationalized by the Czech Communist government. Since 1990, the company has been privatized. Moser is now the largest and most important art glass producer in the Czech Republic, making elaborate, beautifully cut tableware.

Harrach

The Harrach Factory, of Neuwelt, centuries old, is less well known. During the late nineteenth and early twentieth centuries, Harrach made art glass in most of the styles done at Loetz and Moser, as well as cameo glass similar to French Art Nouveau. The quality of much of the glass is equal to that of Loetz and Moser. Harrach rarely signed its glass.

This factory continued to produce glass through the Communist period. In the 1950s, it produced Harrtil, which is often confused with the Seguso Company's Merletto lace glass. Harrtil is occasionally found at antiques shows and malls.

The Cambridge Glass Company

Known for the distinctive jewellike colors of its elegant glass, Cambridge produced more than forty documented colors, from Amethyst to Varitone. Incorporated in 1901 and located in Cambridge, Ohio, the company used in excess of five thousand molds for pressed glass, in addition to its production of blown, etched, and engraved work.

Learn More About Cambridge
Read:
Colors in Cambridge Glass, National Cambridge Collectors, Inc.

Join:
National Cambridge Collectors, Inc.

Visit:
Cambridge Glass Museum

Cambridge used at least five different marks, but not all of its production was marked. National Cambridge Collectors, Inc., have documented most of the output. The company ceased production in 1954 and sold its molds to Imperial, a competitor in Bellaire, Ohio, which also absorbed the rival glassworks of Heisey and Central.

Steuben Glass

Another major American art glass company, Steuben was founded in 1903 in Corning, New York, by Frederick Carder and Thomas H.G. Hawkes. Carder was one of England's top glass artisans and was recruited to the United States.

Carder was not independently wealthy, so he had to make sure his glass was highly commercial in style. He made glass that looked similar to—but not exactly like—Tiffany, as well as Chinese-inspired glass, a Venetian series, cut intaglio glass, Art Deco cameo glass, and much more.

In 1932, Steuben Glass became part of Corning Glass. Carder was retained as artistic director and had his own studio, where he continued to work for many years. But the Steuben Glass factory made only clear sculptural glass from then on.

The Steuben Glass factory is still going strong today. Corning has become a conglomerate of more than forty companies, most specializing in high performance glass and ceramic products for the telecommunications, electronics, optical, and aerospace industries. Corning established the world's greatest glass museum, which is open to the public in Corning, New York. Seminars are held annually for glass scholars and collectors.

Steuben sorbet dish
and saucer, signed,
c. 1910–1920.
Courtesy of
Collector's
Showcase.

> ### *Learn More About Steuben and Corning*
> **Read:**
> *Frederick Carder: Portrait of a Glassmaker.* Paul V. Gardner
>
> *Steuben: Seventy Years of American Glassmaking,* Paul Perrot, Paul Gardner, and James S. Plaut
>
> *American Glass, 1760–1930,* Toledo Museum of Art, vols 1 & 2, Kenneth Wilson
>
> **Visit:**
> Chrysler Museum of Art
>
> Corning Museum of Glass
>
> Toledo Museum of Art

Venetian Glass

Venice and the island of Murano, a few miles out to sea from Venice, are the home of legendary glass factories. This has been the cradle of European glass since the Renaissance.

Salviati & Company

In 1866, a Venetian lawyer, Antonio Salviati, formed a joint company with various prominent British backers. This ushered in an era of color and improvisation in English as well as Venetian, glass. Art glass made during the late Victorian period in the United States and Britain was greatly influenced by Salviati glass.

Salviati glass is colorful, fanciful, light, and fluid in feeling. The glass is all blown, not molded. No two pieces are the same. It is not at all precise like traditional British glass. The techniques of *filigrana* and *millefiore* are used extensively.

Salviati glass was popular until World War II, when it lost favor. It became popular again in the 1990s. Not much of it is signed and many other companies made—and still make—the

> ### *Learn More About Venetian Glass*
> **Read:**
> *The Art of Glass: Art Nouveau to Art Deco,* Victor Arwas
>
> *Venetian Glass, Confections in Glass 1855-1914,* Sheldon Barr
>
> *Art of the Barovier, 1866–1972: Glassmakers in Murano,* Marina Barovier
>
> *Art Glass from Murano, 1910-1970,* Marc Heiremans
>
> **Visit:**
> Corning Museum of Glass

same kind of glass. It is hard to determine age. But it is beautiful and uplifting in style.

Paolo Venini

A lawyer from Como, Italy, son of a glass-blowing family, Paolo Venini "invaded" Murano in the 1920s. He opened a new glassworks and introduced designers from outside Murano, including Gio Ponti. In the 1950s, Venini hired Scandinavian artists such as the Finn Tapio Wirkkala. These imported designers were to create a whole new vocabulary for Murano glass factories.

Venini glass became so popular with the avant garde and was so successful financially that traditional Murano families started to copy it. Venini continued to be a leading influence, not only on Murano glass, but also on international styles, through the 1960s.

Barovier

One of the most successful and talented of the traditional Murano glassmaking families is Barovier. Different branches of

Vase with mille-fiore. Artisans produce the flower-like patterns of millefiore (from the Italian *mille fiori,* a thousand flowers) by cross-cutting multicolored bundles of glass rods.

39

the large family, with slightly different names, have worked in glass for over eight hundred years, and still do.

After Venini changed the rules—as well as the styles—of the glassmaking game in Murano, Ercole Barovier created his own new masterpieces. He worked from the 1920s through the 1960s. His pieces can be light or massive, but they are all gorgeously colorful and technically brilliant.

Studio Glass

The studio glass movement was begun in 1962 by two American artists, Harvey Littleton and Domenic Labino. Littleton devised a small glass oven that enabled artists to work in individual studios. The studio movement has swept across the world since then. Glassmaking schools such as Pilchuck, outside Seattle, Washington, have opened (Pilchuck was started by studio artist Dale Chihuly). Many universities have glassmaking departments.

Dale Chihuly

Dale Chihuly is the most influential of today's American studio glassmakers. He has often been compared to Tiffany. Chihuly is American, but was trained in Murano, Italy, and does many large-scale, Venetian-inspired, colorful, contemporary installations as

---

Learn More About Studio Glass
Read:
New Glass: A Worldwide Survey, Corning Museum Staff

Contemporary Glass: A World Survey from the Corning Museum of Glass, Susanne K. Frantz

Contemporary Art Glass, Ray Grover and Lee Grover

Out of the Fire: Contemporary Glass Artists and Their Work, Bonnie J. Miller

Visit:
Corning Museum of Art

The Renwick Museum, Washington, D.C.

The American Craft Museum, New York, NY

---

well as small works suitable for private homes. His work is in many art museums and public buildings. He is known all over the world. While he started as a studio artist, he now works factory-style with a team and large furnaces. He, like Tiffany, designs and directs the work. He makes both one-of-a-kind pieces and series of up to two thousand pieces. One well-known series is called the Persians.

Chihuly's work is sold in glass galleries and resold in auction houses. In the late 1990s, Chihuly founded Portland Press, which is exclusive publisher of many books, exhibition catalogs, videos, and other products associated with his work.

Stevens & Williams
rock crystal cut bowl.
See page 70.

BEFORE YOU START COLLECTING

It's natural to want to rush right out and begin your collection immediately, but the more prepared you are, the more successful you'll be. In this section, longtime collectors and dealers provide you with guidelines they wish they'd had when they started out and offer advice they learned through long and sometimes painful experience.

The Golden Rules of Collecting

Buy Only What You Like

The cardinal rule of collecting is to buy what you like and know something about. It's often tempting to speculate about buying as an investment. This is folly for all but the most experienced glass experts. One appraiser of elegant glass cautions, "The best collections have the strong imprint of the owner's taste. The worst collections are those on which money was spent in hopes of a rising market."

Learn All You Can First

Read, research, and look at every glass collection you can. Go to shows just to look and learn, study catalogs, and talk to other collectors. "Antiques Roadshow" and similar television programs are good sources of information, and there are new specialized online sources appearing all the time.

Authoritative books are your best resource, and you should consider the task of building your reference library to be as important as making your first glass purchases. Be wary of untrustworthy sources; ask seasoned collectors for their recommendations. Some books may contain inaccuracies, yet have merit because they tackle types of glass otherwise ignored. When a book is thought by others to be "iffy," cross-check any information you glean from it with other sources.

Also be careful with auction catalogs. Remember: They were produced by auction houses trying to attain the highest possible prices. Sotheby's and Christie's catalogs of recent years are pretty reliable in terms of descriptions, but the estimated prices can be misleading. Likewise, the prices-realized list—usually available after the auction to purchasers of the catalog—may reflect the results of bidding wars between two individuals determined to walk away with the prize, regardless of the cost.

Both novices and experienced collectors may find themselves in a quandary when faced with misinformation in the marketplace. Erroneous information may be propagated through ignorance or by intent, but it is everywhere. *Always use multiple sources to verify:* books, magazines, trade papers, videos, other collectors. If you've done your research before you begin buying, you'll know when something is not right—and exactly where you can go to find the facts.

COLLECTOR'S COMPASS

Be an informed buyer. If, for example, you are collecting Depression Glass in Jeannette's "Cherry Blossom" pattern, you'd better research the following questions:

- What items were originally produced in that pattern?
- What colors were made? Were all items made in each color?
- What were the years of production?

When you have your facts down cold, you won't be misled into purchasing a fake or a reproduction.

The Price Is Right

Study all the books you can find on your chosen glass specialty, including price guides. But never rely completely on a price guide. Compare the information in the guide with information from other sources:

- Check out the prices of similar pieces at antiques malls and shows
- Read the ads in trade magazines and newspapers
- Talk to other collectors with similar interests, including those in other geographic areas
- Review completed auctions on eBay and other Internet auction services to see what similar pieces brought under competitive bidding situations. Review the bid history. This sometimes gives you a sense of how high the interest in a piece may be.

Stay within Your Budget

A collection can grow as rapidly or as slowly as your resources allow. Don't buy solely as an investment, because there are no guarantees that glass will appreciate. Generally, antiques and collectibles have not been a reliable investment for the last fifteen years. If, for instance, you bought a piece of art glass fifteen years ago at market price, chances are its value has increased only slightly. (There are exceptions, such as many Tiffany items.)

If you are able to buy glass that you enjoy at less than market price, then you will be ahead of the game. That's why yard sales and flea markets are so popular. But be careful in competitive situations such as auctions. It's easy to get carried away in the heat of bidding and forget all about your budget. Decide in advance what your limit is, and stick to it.

Look for Quality, Not Quantity

Most experts advise that you'll be more successful over the long run, and happier with your collection, if you buy the best pieces you can. For example, a single piece of Cambridge Caprice glassware in mint condition is a smarter purchase than five pieces that show wear. A rare piece, even one in imperfect condition, is the only exception. Be sure of its scarcity or of the impossibility of affording a piece in mint condition before settling for an inferior example. It's very unlikely to appreciate in value.

Honor Your Commitments

Be a considerate collector. Don't return a purchase unless it was misrepresented in some way. If you do return something, do it as soon as possible, certainly within a few days of your purchase or receipt. If you're bidding in on-line auctions, be prompt and communicative in sending payments to sellers; if you're not, you risk getting negative feedback. Once your profile is besmirched, other sellers and buyers may decide not to do business with you. You risk having your bids cancelled and, worse, being suspended from bidding altogether.

Be a Friendly Competitor

Share information with other collectors. It's the best way to learn more about your chosen specialty. And you're more likely to get leads about a piece of glass for your collection from competitors who already own a similar piece. In turn, give leads to others.

Join a Collectors' Club

By joining collectors' groups and glass societies, you can learn more about your common interests with others and also pass on knowledge you have acquired.

One collector began with a specific Cambridge tableware pattern and then became interested in everything about the manufacturer. So he joined the National Cambridge Collectors' Society. He states: "As a member, I receive a monthly newsletter with articles on Cambridge glassware and have an opportunity to attend the society's annual convention each year in Cambridge, Ohio. These conventions are an excellent place to learn *everything* about Cambridge glass."

Be Patient

Once you've decided to start a collection or expand into a new area, the natural inclination is to buy, buy, buy, and watch that collection grow! However, rushing into premature purchases may cause you to sacrifice quality, to overpay, or to lose sight of your original goal.

If you've started a collection of Sabino animal figurines and have purchased two or three, enjoy them for awhile. Make sure you still like them. Meanwhile, learn everything there is to know about Sabino, decide exactly what pieces you want, and budget for future purchases.

Surround Yourself with Your Collection

A happy collector is surrounded by his or her collection. Give some consideration to available space—it may help you decide what type of glass you want to collect (goblets will require less space than bowls). All the experts say you have to be able to display your collection where you can view it daily in order to truly enjoy it.

Develop Relationships with Dealers

Go to shows and meet dealers who sell what you collect. Tell them what you're seeking. Give them your phone number, take their cards, and call once in a while to ask if they've found anything.

It takes time and effort to establish a relationship, but once a dealer knows you'll buy from her, she'll watch out for items that will interest you and show them to you first.

A Step-by-Step Guide to the Marketplace

What to Look for in Art Glass and Studio Glass

Art glass offers you a greater potential for undiscovered treasure than elegant glass, because the latter is a long-established collectible whose value is recognized by more people. To find bargains, you must first explore the perimeters of what most people look for in art glass.

One likely area is contemporary work. *Don't* try to find undiscovered pieces by Dale Chihuly, the most famous contemporary artist. Instead, look for the work of less-well-known glass artists, especially from the late 1960s and 1970s. Studio glass was a new medium in the United States then, and many excellent artisans from that era are still relatively unknown.

American glass artists usually dated and signed or initialed their work. A few of the early studio signatures you might want to look for are Labino, Littleton, Peiser, Dreisbach, Nygren, Ritter, and Thiewes. Glasswork in the 1960s and 1970s was less sophisticated than glassware of today. Most examples were vessels in form, although small sculptures were also made.

European studio glass was also usually signed. Two notable exceptions are glass made in Murano, Italy, which had paper labels that came off, and much of the wonderful Czech sculptural glass. Unless you have an expert with you who can identify unsigned work or you find something so gorgeous and irresistible you simply *must* have it, begin a collection with signed pieces. Signed pieces will always be more important than unsigned pieces because they can be authenticated. Early studio glass is good to collect because the glass is usually signed, signatures have not yet begun to be faked, the glass is new enough not to have much damage, and prices are reasonable.

Danish glass made by the artist Per Lütken for Holmegaards Glasværks during the 1950s and 1960s is still reasonably priced and is an icon of mid-twentieth-century style. This glass, usually either smoky or pale blue, is curvaceous and even biomorphic in design (for example, echoing the ubiquitous kidney-shaped coffee tables of the era). It is always signed *PL,* with the company name and a date and sometimes even a model number. There was a great deal of this glass made, although no two pieces are identical. A lot is still available, and you may even find it at flea markets.

Although eBay has created quite a market for twentieth-century designer glass from Finland, the glass can still be found as an undiscovered treasure. The signatures are hard to read and unfamiliar. The three factories are Iittala (the most familiar), Nuutajarvi, and Riihimaki. Some

Iittala "Cog" vase, designed by Tapio Wirkkala, 8" high. *Photo courtesy of Wright.*

continued on page 65

20th Century Glass Photo Gallery

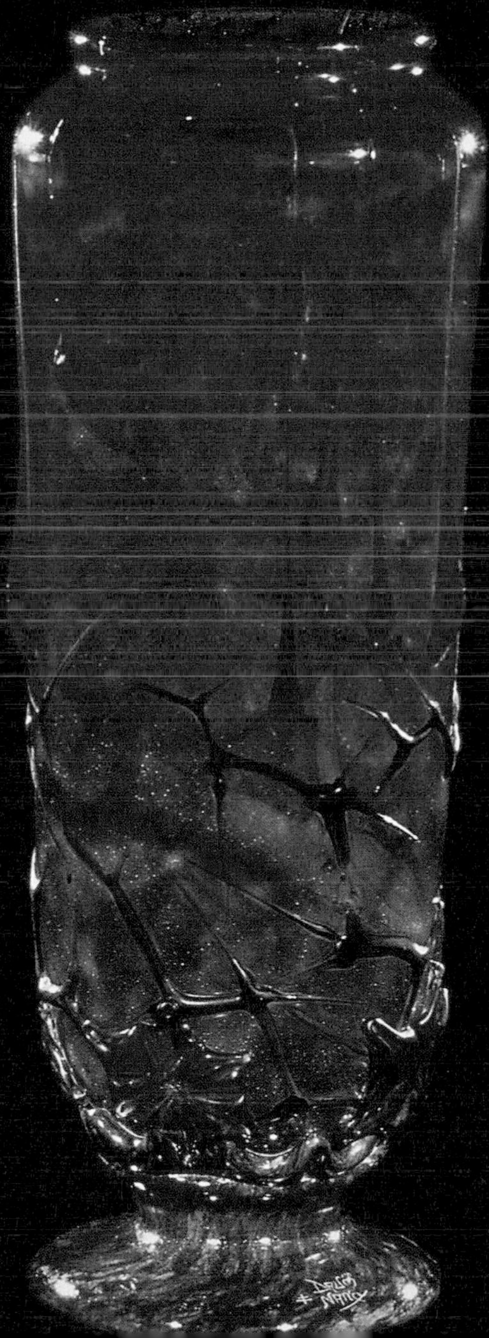

Cristalleries Daum
"Crown of Thorns"
vase; Nancy, France;
22½" high; c. 1911.
© The Corning
Museum of Glass.

Ludwig Moser &
Söhne Company
pedestal vases
designed by Ludwig
Moser; Karlsbad,
Bohemia; 31⅜"
high (tallest); 1880–
1890. © *The Corning
Museum of Glass.*

Studio of Emile Gallé vase; Nancy,
France; 11¹⁄₁₆" high; c. 1910.
© *The Corning Museum of Glass.*

Artisti Barovier
vase designed
by Vittorio
Zecchin;
Venice, Italy;
18 7/8" high;
c. 1914.
© The Corning
Museum of
Glass.

Barovier and Toso
"Intarsio" bowl
designed by Ercole
Barovier; Murano,
Italy; 4 3/4" high, 6 3/8"
diameter; 1964–1965.
© The Corning
Museum of Glass.

Emile Gallé vase;
Nancy, France;
4 11/16" high;
1885–1900. © The
Corning Museum
of Glass.

Vase designed by Ercole Barovier; Murano, Italy; 7⅞" high; c. 1950. © The Corning Museum of Glass.

"Victoire" automobile hood ornament by René Lalique, France, 1928–1947. © The Corning Museum of Glass.

"Pissenlit" vase by René Lalique; France; 5¾" high, 7" deep; c. 1926. © The Corning Museum of Glass.

Steuben iridescent blue fluted vase, 5" high, United States, c. 1920. *Courtesy of Collector's Showcase.*

Louis Comfort Tiffany fruit cup and saucer, United States, iridescent blue and amber, c. 1920. *Courtesy of Collector's Showcase.*

Louis Comfort Tiffany favrile centerpiece; 10" diameter, 2½" high; c. 1900. This centerpiece features a removable, two-level flower frog in the middle for holding stems. *Courtesy of Collector's Showcase.*

53

Left: Venini and Company flute glass designed by Paolo Venini; 18½" high, 9½" deep; c. 1975. © The Corning Museum of Glass.

Right: Homegaards Glasværk bottles designed by Per Lütken Copenhagen, Denmark; 15" high (tallest). © The Corning Museum of Glass.

Iittala "Chantarelle" glass designed by Tapio Wirkkala. From left to right: 4½" high vase, 7½" long dish, 13" high vase, 10" high vase. *Photo courtesy of Wright.*

Right: Venini and Cie "Fazzoletto" bowl; Murano, Italy; 9⅜"; c. 1950. © The Corning Museum of Glass.

Homegaards Glasværk "Provence" bowl designed by Per Lütken; Copenhagen, Denmark; 6¼" high, 10½" diameter; c. 1956. *© The Corning Museum of Glass.*

Kosta vases, Sweden, 1950s, from left to right: designed by Vicke Lindstrand, 9"
high; "Ventana" designed by Monica Morales-Schildt, 6½" high; "Colora"
designed by Vicke Lindstrand, 13" high; designed by Monica Morales-Schildt, 8"
high. *Photo courtesy of Wright.*

Kosta vases designed by
Vicke Lindstrand, Sweden,
1950s, from left to right:
"Trees in Fog," 9½" high;
"Autumn," 6½" high;
"Abstracta," 12" high.
Photo courtesy of Wright.

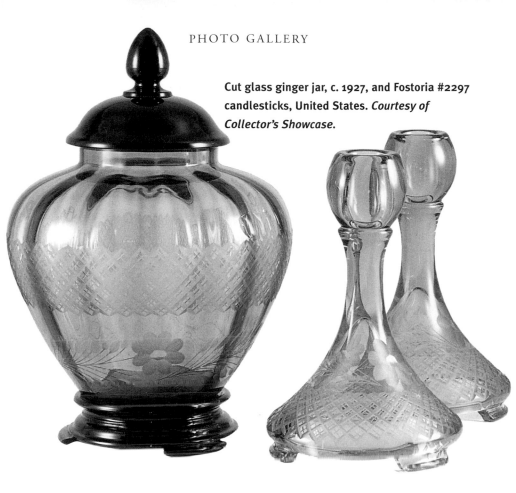

Cut glass ginger jar, c. 1927, and Fostoria #2297 candlesticks, United States. *Courtesy of Collector's Showcase.*

Compote, unsigned, United States, c. 1910–1920. *Courtesy of Collector's Showcase.*

Left: Fenton "Big Cookies" mandarin basket with woven bamboo handle, United States, c. 1933. Below: Fenton Mongolian basket weave bowl, United States, c. 1935. *Courtesy of Collector's Showcase.*

Heisey "Crystolite" bowl with the distinctive "Diamond H" mark on the bottom.

Fostoria blue-stemmed water goblets, 8-piece set; United States; 1920–1930. *Courtesy of Star Center Mall.*

Fenton cased lilac pitcher, United States, c. 1955. *Courtesy of Collector's Showcase.*

Duncan Miller peach opalescent "Sylvan" swan, 12" high, 12" wide; c. 1940s. *Courtesy of Collector's Showcase.*

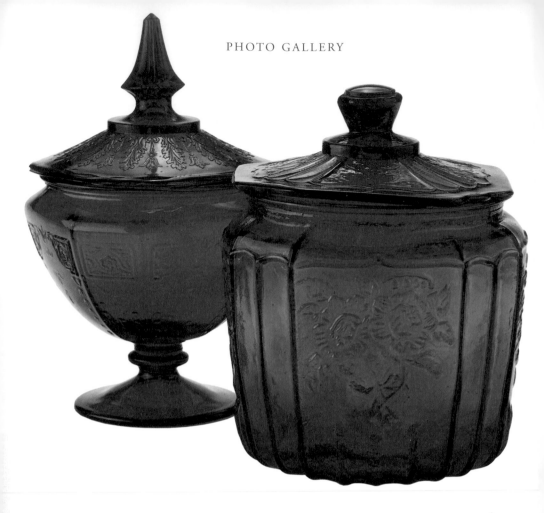

Hocking Glass Company Depression glass. Left: "Princess" candy jar with lid (reproduction Depression glass), United States, 1931–1934. "Princess" was made in pink, green, yellow, topaz, blue (shown), and satinized pink and green. Right: Mayfair "Open Rose" cookie jar with lid, United States, 1931–1936. Mayfair was made in blue (shown), crystal, green, pink, yellow, and satinized pink and blue.

Left: Cambridge Glass Company Depression glass. "Caprice" creamer, sugar, and tray; United States; 1936– 1958. "Caprice" was made in amber, amethyst, emerald green, cobalt blue, crystal, pink, moonlight blue (shown), and white.

Jeannette Glass Company Depression glass. "Cherry Blossom" pitcher with round base, United States, 6¾" high, 1930–1939. "Cherry Blossom" was made in crystal, delphite, green, jade-ite, pink (shown), red, and yellow.

Cambridge Glass Company Depression glass. "Rosepoint" candlestick, goblet, and dish; United States; 1936–1953. "Rosepoint" was made in amber, black, blue, Crown Tuscan, crystal (shown), and red.

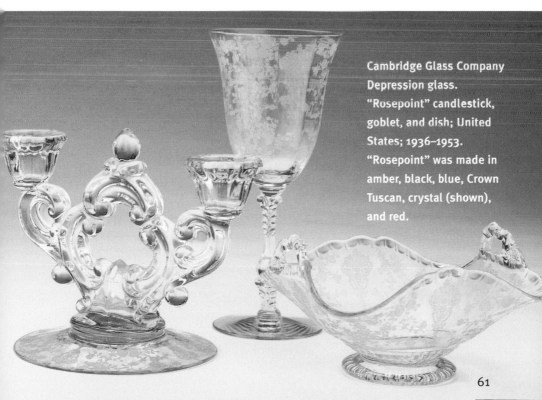

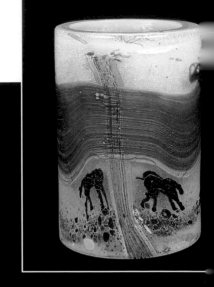

Right: "Double Saddle Blanket" by Dale Chihuly with the assistance of Flora Mace; United States; 8 3/16" high, 5 3/8" diameter; c. 1975. © *The Corning Museum of Glass.*

Below left: Stoppered bottle with "Camouflage-Toe" Ghost Frogs designed and made by John Fergus Nygren; United States; 8 11/16" high, 3 3/4" wide, 2 15/16" deep; c. 1983. © *The Corning Museum of Glass.*

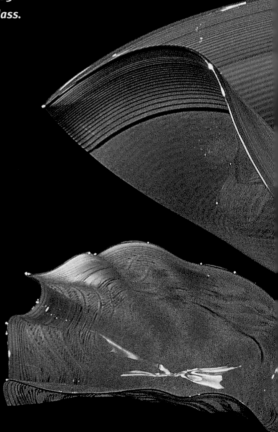

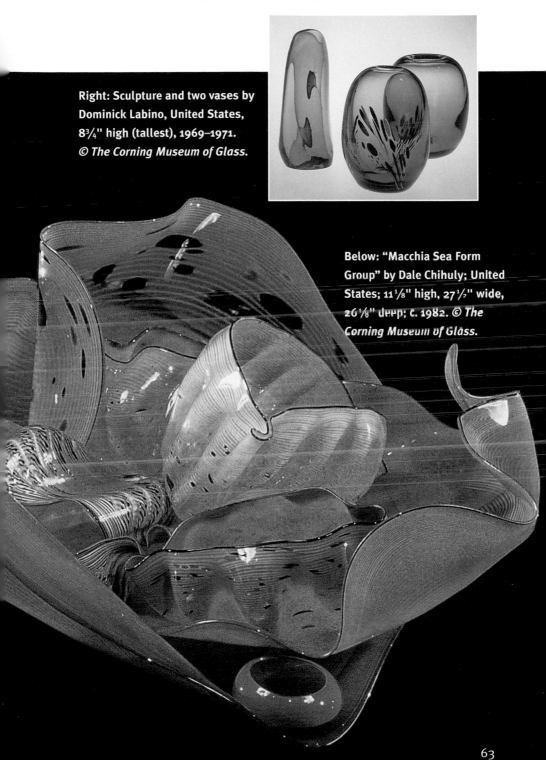

Right: Sculpture and two vases by Dominick Labino, United States, 8¾" high (tallest), 1969–1971. © *The Corning Museum of Glass.*

Below: "Macchia Sea Form Group" by Dale Chihuly; United States; 11⅛" high, 27½" wide, 26⅛" deep; c. 1982. © *The Corning Museum of Glass.*

Above: Cup designed and made by John Nygren, United States, 3⅜" high, c. 1977. © *The Corning Museum of Glass.*

Above: "Family Portrait" by Richard Q. Ritter, Jr.; United States; 6¾" high, 8¼" diameter; c. 1976. © *The Corning Museum of Glass.*

Below: "Wisteria" by Mark C. Peiser; United States; 8¾" high, 8¼" diameter; c. 1976. © *The Corning Museum of Glass.*

continued from page 48

Finnish glass carried paper labels that have come off, so you'll need to know the shapes that were made; some are quite distinctive. There is a long list of designers and artists, led by Tapio Wirkkala and Timo Sarpeneva.

What to Look for in Elegant and Depression-Era Glass

While a satisfying collection of art or studio glass may be built of a handful of stunning, beautifully designed pieces, most collectors of elegant tableware set out to build place settings and eventually full services of their favorite patterns and colors. The many highly specialized serving dishes typical of the period (celery dish, nappy, fruit bowl, covered preserve, and so on) add to the quest. And décor pieces—such as console sets (candelabra and comports), vanity items, and lamp bases and vases—can carry one's preferred pattern throughout the home.

All the companies that made elegant glass had several pattern lines that are desirable to collectors and command top dollar today. Heisey's Orchid and Rose and Cambridge's Rosepoint are examples of popular etched patterns that are readily recognized by all dealers, who realize they will bring full retail price.

So after studying the reference books on the wares of these companies, you might want to select an etching you like that isn't in as much demand as the "hot" patterns. Or, collect less popular colors. You can find patterns or blanks in amber and yellow that will be much less expensive than the same patterns in blue or red.

Perhaps you like many of the patterns that were made and can't decide on a particular one. Consider collecting sherbet dishes or cup-and-saucer sets in different patterns and colors. These pieces will be less expensive than dinner plates, goblets, or cordials.

Another avenue to consider is collecting "singles" of items usually sold in matched pairs. One collector we know has a lovely grouping of single candlesticks in assorted styles, heights, and colors.

Fenton Glass Company's current production will do nothing but increase in value over the years. Also, Dalzell-Viking has just closed its doors, so prices for its glass will start to move up. And

Fenton cased lilac pitcher, c. 1955. *Courtesy of Collector's Showcase.*

Early American pattern glass has recently taken a dive in popularity, so there's plenty on dealers' shelves waiting for a new home.

If your hunt focuses on finding specific individual pieces, working with established dealers, attending specialized glass shows and auctions, frequenting consignment shops, and poring over ads listed in trade papers and on-line auctions will net you the best return on your time invested. You must pay close to market value in almost all cases; a heated auction for a much-desired piece could run the price much higher.

Bargains are possible around the fringes of the secondary market—garage and tag sales, flea markets, charity bazaars, and estate sales. But here you're fair game for fakes and reproductions, and the condition of the glassware you're likely to find is often less than perfect. Or you may have to buy a large lot of pieces in order to get the one or few you really want.

Let's face it: professional dealers know where to look for new material coming into the market, and their pickers are out every day making a living by snapping up the desirable pieces before they get into individual collectors' hands. The casual weekend bargain hunter is going to find glass, but it's likely to be the "leavings" after the pros have already skimmed off the choice stuff (estate auctions are the exception, as we'll see on page 69). If you consider weekend hunting a form of recreation, go ahead and have fun. But be prepared to be out early in the morning and to come up empty-handed much of the time.

Garage, Yard, and Tag Sales

You'll find glass in abundance at garage and yard sales in most areas of the country, but as we noted, a lot of it is junk. One collector who eventually became a dealer touts the rewards of digging through used clothing and baby toys to uncover the occasional "treasure." He urges new collectors to try every type of sale at least once as part of your education in glass. You'll decide soon enough which venues you prefer to shop.

When you read the classifieds to plan your itinerary, check ads for the wealthiest towns and neighborhoods in your area. The richest people have the best stuff, and that's likely to include glass. When you set off for the day, take boxes and packing materials. It is also a good idea to take plenty of cash along; most people won't take checks. Carry a supply of printed or handwritten cards with your name, contact information, and the type of glass you are looking for, and don't forget to take your favorite glass reference book along (to check marks or signatures, or to compare a find to the photo).

While you're rummaging through the tables, ask the proprietor if there is any other glass that hasn't been put out yet. You'll be surprised how many people will bring out more! Or someone may tell you they have other glass they're not planning to sell now. Give the owner your card and tell her you'd appreciate the chance to see it if she ever decides to sell.

If you want an item that you think is overpriced, ask the owner politely if the price is negotiable. Decide in advance how much you're prepared to pay, and explain why you think it's fair. Many people have no idea *what* they're selling, and tend to price something higher if they think it's "pretty" but know nothing more about it.

If you've selected quite a few items at one garage sale, ask the owner for a quantity discount. Customarily, this may amount to 10 to 15 percent, but not everyone bites. If no discount is forthcoming, you'll have to decide if the glass is worth the asking price to you.

Tag sales are a little different, since they are usually run by a professional outfit. The tag sale company is brought in to organize, price, and advertise the sale. Often you must line up at daybreak in order to get a number. And thanks to their preferential relationships with the tag sale company, usually local dealers will have had first crack long before you even heard about the sale.

Ordinarily, at tag sales you purchase at the price marked. You have the option to offer a lower bid, and if the item hasn't been sold by the end of the sale, the manager will contact the highest bidder.

Flea Markets

Glass of every variety and description can be found in abundance at virtually all flea markets, but remember that there is no jurying of the merchandise. People can sell anything they choose in whatever condition and call it whatever they wish. It's up to you to determine its true market value. A lot of fakes show up in flea markets, so examine things closely. Be discerning. Try to see each item as it is, not as you'd like it to be. A longtime collector suggests that you restrain the urge to buy during your first flea market visits—just look, learn, and examine until you can authenticate the type of glass you want to buy.

Once you're confident enough to shop for real, arrive early while some of the dealers are still setting up. Talk to them, leave your card, and tell them what you're looking for. They may save pieces for you if they know you'll be back every Sunday.

Opportunities for haggling are greater at flea markets than at garage or tag sales. Most dealers expect—even encourage—some back-and-forth over prices, especially if it's done in good humor. You can usually negotiate a 10 to 15–percent discount, a little more if you're buying in large quantity.

Bazaars
Bazaars are usually held by churches, synagogues, and civic groups and can be a productive source of glass. It's a hit-and-miss venture, though, as you'll never know in advance which bazaar will have the mother lode of Carnival glass and which will have not so much as a perfume bottle.

Bargains are possible because the volunteers doing the pricing often don't know the value of many categories of donated items. You shouldn't ask for a discount at a charity bazaar, but occasionally you may be offered one by a good-natured volunteer if you're buying in quantity.

Thrift and Consignment Shops
Charity thrift shops—whose proceeds benefit community agencies, hospitals, cancer research, and so on—often have professional appraisers on staff. Prices tend to be high, as the nonprofit shop keeps a big percentage of the sale, sometimes 30 or 40 percent. Consequently, our experts say that glass prices in upscale second-hand shops are sometimes *twice* the going antique show prices. Of course, if you want to both support the charity and treat yourself to a lovely glass figurine, this is a great way to do both. Just don't assume that "thrift" means cheap.

For-profit thrift shops usually require you to wade through a lot of junk before you get to any glass that might be there. Many collectors think these shops are a waste of time, but at least scout out the ones in your town before you dismiss them. Prices at for-profit thrift shops, unlike at nonprofit shops, should be negotiable.

Some shops reduce prices after an item has been in stock for a month.

Consignment shops may be a good place to buy glass (or even a good place to sell when you upgrade your collection). Consignment shops charge the seller a percentage of the selling price, so it's to their benefit to get the most they can for the items. But they need frequent inventory turnover, so ask if prices are negotiable. Some shop owners may flatly refuse, but others will be willing to contact the owner to negotiate a price. Be prepared to make a reasonable offer on the spot.

Most consignment shops automatically reduce prices after a specified time—thirty or sixty days, for instance—to make way for new merchandise. If you're interested in an item, ask when the price will be reduced.

Estate Sales and Auctions

Most glass aficionados have stories about the wonderful pieces they've found at estate sales and auctions and recommend this venue to new collectors. But they also warn of some pitfalls.

First, *never* assume that estate glass is high quality just because of the highfalutin term. It may not even be desirable.

Second, attending estate sales is very time consuming. Collectors all have horror stories of driving a distance, waiting outside the house in the blazing heat or freezing rain with a number, and then finding that all the glass of collectible value was gone.

Another warning: estate sale prices are not necessarily bargains. Buyers often think they are and sometimes pay too much.

Despite these caveats, most collectors have a personal preference for estate sales, where an entire household is being liquidated and there's apt to be glass. Many were thrilled to find the best pieces they own at excellent prices, but hunting down these sales is not for the faint of heart.

Estate auctions usually attract swarms of dealers who are competing for the same items you are. But you have the advantage! A dealer who is going to resell a Morgantown Colette compote for seventy dollars can invest only about thirty dollars in acquiring it. But if forty or forty-five dollars seems like a good price to you, it makes you and the seller happy.

Antiques and Collectibles Malls

Antiques and collectibles malls are fun to shop in, although it is rare to find anything spectacular in them. When a special item

The Devil is in the Details

The Stevens & Williams rock crystal bowl shown here was probably designed by Frederick Carder when he worked there. He and T. G. Hawkes later founded the Steuben Glass Company in 1903. It's unlikely that estate appraisers will know of the connection; thus, you may find such a bowl underpriced if you know what to look for. The Carder/Steuben connection greatly increases the value of the bowl to a collector.

Incidentally, bowls—even rare ones like this—are frequently found at estate sales. They do not command the prices of vases because they take up so much space. So, if you have oodles of room, bowls would be a great specialty for you. Noncollectors who are simply looking for a beautiful bowl to use won't spend a lot of money, so a savvy collector can have a champagne collection on a beer budget.

comes in, another dealer in the mall generally sees it first and nabs it.

Nonetheless, many collectors love to shop in malls. One reports, "My favorite haunt for elegant glassware is antiques malls. If I'm fortunate enough to locate a rare or scarce piece that is way underpriced, I get a mental high knowing that I found it before someone else!"

Each booth or showcase in an antiques mall is rented from the management by a separate dealer; some dealers pay a commission on sales, as well. In turn, mall personnel manage the sales of the merchandise when the dealers are not there.

Some mall owners are selective about whom they invite into their malls, barring fakes, fantasy items (pieces attributed to a particular designer or maker that were never made by them), and reproductions (current production pieces made by the original manufacturer, often from original molds). In other malls, you're likely to find a lot of misrepresented items and salespeople who haven't a clue about the merchandise. Be wary, and be sure you *know* what you're buying.

Individual Shops and Galleries

There are fewer and fewer independent antique glass shops because overhead is too steep for all but high-end items. When you find an antiques shop specializing in glass, the dealer will be knowledgeable about his or her merchandise. Not only can you learn a great deal from the dealer, if you're a good customer, you'll have someone who's willing to keep an eye out for your "want list." Prices in antiques shops may be negotiable, but don't expect bargains. Top quality and rare pieces are likely to surface in specialty shops. They won't be cheap, and dealers have little reason to discount prices considering that their desirability usually almost assures a quick turnover.

COLLECTOR'S COMPASS

Negotiating the best price you can get is smart, but never ever try to get the price reduced by criticizing the merchandise. What dealer is going to negotiate a better price for someone who responds, "That's a ridiculous price for this piece of junk"? Try instead, "I'm willing to pay X dollars for an item in this condition," or "It's really lovely, but prices are down because there's so much Carnival on the market now. I can't invest that much in one plate," as acceptable negotiating tactics. You will show that you're both courteous and knowledgeable.

There are more and more galleries specializing in contemporary art glass. Unlike the other venues discussed here, galleries are a primary, rather than secondary, market, and prices are not negotiable. Medium-range galleries carry fine-quality work; their supply of glass usually comes from the major craft fairs, where artists rent booths and sell at wholesale prices to galleries and at retail prices directly to the public.

Fenton glass on display at Collector's Showcase, a specialty shop in Snohomish, Washington.

Antiques and Collectibles Shows

The big antiques shows are probably the best place for a beginner to start. You can see and handle hundreds if not thousands of pieces of glass of different kinds, compare prices, talk to the dealers and other collectors, and enjoy the ambiance.

When you're ready to begin buying for your collection, try to get an experienced collector friend to join you at a show. Once you've walked through several of the large shows and made a few purchases with the help of your tagalong expert, it will be far easier to shop on your own. You'll begin to know how to size up dealers' reliability, how to focus on one object at a time, and how to negotiate a price.

Always have the dealer write out any verbal guarantees on the sales receipt. Be sure you have his or her name and contact information. The sales receipt should say what the item is; the date made, if known; the signature, if any; anything else the dealer says is important about the piece; and the price paid. If the dealer won't write it down, don't believe it.

Glass Shows

Specialized glass shows are the best place to find all types of glass in quantity and depth. The dealers usually save their best pieces for such shows and would not dare offer fakes, reproductions, or altered glass.

These shows are the safest place for a novice collector to shop. The majority of the dealers travel from one show to the next,

---

Prices, Prices

Dealers arrive at their prices in a number of ways. Some dealers price their wares based solely on what they paid for each piece. Some base prices on the current market. Still others base them on what they see in other dealers' booths. Most use a combination of these factors. You want to be a regular customer of the dealer who takes into account the rarity and condition of the individual piece, its desirability, and the prevailing market value, as well as the dealer's cost.

Many dealers build in a 10- to 15-percent discount. In other words, they anticipate that you'll ask for a discount, so they set prices high enough to give you one while still maintaining their profit.

Occasionally, you'll encounter dealers who don't put prices on their merchandise, preferring to have you ask. Be wary of this practice. Some experts advise that you not patronize such dealers, who "size up" customers and charge whatever they think the traffic will bear.

---

selling glass in different areas of the country. They know their inventory, have researched their glass, and will disclose any flaws or damage.

The show managers, most likely glass collectors themselves, will try to vary the offerings, with booths that specialize in American art glass, European art glass, pressed glass, Early American pattern glass, Depression glass, contemporary glass, paperweights, perfume bottles, and so on, as well as books—new and out of print—on every subject related to glass.

There are even shows featuring one kind of glass. There is an all-Heisey show. There are Depression glass shows. There are shows that specialize in one style, such as the Modernism Show, which includes fine twentieth-century glass, and the Art Deco Show, where you can see Art Deco glass.

Glass shows are not the best place for bargains because they are so competitive, but they are a must for new collectors. The extraordinary range of glass to admire, the assurance of authenticity, and the opportunity to see pieces you'll probably never see elsewhere are unparalleled. They're great shows for experienced collectors, too, because of the sought-after rarities that may be found.

Glass shows are important to new collectors for another reason, as well. A number of them are sponsored by collectors' societies that provide educational bonuses. For instance, the annual International Perfume Bottle Convention conducts workshops and seminars. No matter how many books you read, you can't replicate the value of attending these programs. You'll not only hobnob with the top experts, you'll meet fellow novice collectors, participate in a special catalog auction featuring the finest perfume bottles, and be admitted to a members-only preview of the show and a "bargain" sale for members only.

Dealer Fixed-Price Catalogs and Auctions

Some dealers send out mail-order catalogs or run independent mail and telephone auctions of glass. In theory, a fixed price is a fair price because it's the same for everyone on a first-come-first-served basis, but that alone doesn't make it a good value. Be cautious.

Several of our experts advise that you avoid these mail or telephone sales for the simple reason that glass should be carefully examined before you buy. Most mail-order lists have one-sentence descriptions, no photos, and rarely mention the condition of the item.

Mailing-list dealers are becoming a rare breed. Most have given up selling this way in favor of doing business on the Internet.

Web Sites and Internet Auctions

You'll find that the Internet is a good place to look. You can see only one item at a time and, therefore, you can focus on it. The lack of distraction is a boon for beginning collectors. There is an amazing amount of glass from which to choose. The biggest drawback is that you cannot handle the pieces.

Some Web sites offer a variety of antiques and collectibles for sale, some offer only glass, and some are set up strictly for glass dealers. Sites such as www.glassshow.com or www.cyberattic.com can be great sources of high-quality, harder-to-find glass. Antiques or glass shops often have Web sites linked to auction sites. The process is simple. When you locate a piece that you're interested in, e-mail the owner and ask *specific* questions about condition, signature, and any other relevant issues. If you decide to buy, save all the seller's e-mails that concern documentation of the piece. You'll need them if it turns out the glass was misrepresented in any way. Send your payment, including shipping costs, and the seller will pack and ship your purchase.

Online auctions are the newest thing and can be a real boon to the collector. The granddaddy of auction sites, www.ebay.com is fun, well established, and relatively safe to use. A number of safeguards have been built into its system, so it's a good place to begin online buying. Procedures for registering to bid and using the site are explained in great detail, so simply follow the prompts from the home page to get set up as a bidder.

Now to the search! Go to the search box and type in a keyword description: *Victorian art glass* or *Fostoria American*, for instance. You will likely find one or more photos of the item for sale, plus a description. Read the description carefully, noting any comments the seller makes about identification, condition, and authenticity. Note the terms of sale and shipping terms (these will vary from seller to seller).

If your questions about a piece are not fully answered by what you see and read, send the seller an e-mail and ask about anything with which you are not fully satisfied. Most sellers will respond promptly; many will attach additional scans to their e-mails to give you details that may have been missing from their original posting (they may add the content of what they send you to the listing, for others to see as well. Don't wait until the last day of the auction to request more information; you may not get a response in time.

If you decide to bid on an object, you scroll down to the bidding directions and make your bid. You'll be told immediately if you're the high bidder or if someone else has outbid you. If you are not the high bidder, you can place a higher bid or elect to "watch this item" on a special "My eBay" area on the site (you can "watch" up to twenty items at a time). It's up to you to keep track of the closing time if you still might want to place a bid.

Many bidders don't bid until the last minutes of the auction. This practice is called "sniping," and it's the subject of heated debate among Internet auction users. As with a live auction, you should set a maximum you're willing to bid and stick to it. Whether you decide to place your maximum bid as soon as you've located a desired item or in the final minutes of an auction, the eBay system will automatically execute bids for you against competitors, at the auction's standard increments, until your maximum is reached. Theoretically and practically, the person who places the highest maximum bid will win, usually by the system's narrow bid increment of a few dollars. Losing by a hairsbreadth can be heartbreaking, but there's fairness in the item's going to the bidder who was willing to risk paying the highest maximum price.

Sometimes, the seller will set a reserve price—a minimum price beneath which he or she will not sell the item. If the bidding does not reach the reserve, the item goes unsold. The item screen in a reserve price auction will always indicate whether the reserve price has or has not been met, but it will not reveal what the reserve actually is.

Keyword Searches

Finding elegant and pattern glass on eBay is pretty straightforward. If you enter the manufacturer and the pattern or type (for example, Greentown Holly Amber or Libbey brilliant cut glass) in the search box you'll obtain a comprehensive listing of current offerings.

On the other hand, you'll need to be imaginative to find keywords that will produce the type of art glass you want to find. Artist's names are seldom found, although a few Scandinavian names will turn up listings. Company names, especially European glass producers, have interminably long lists that are not broken down by subcategory.

Also, try searching for the decade in which the glass was made, such as 1930s; for a style, such as Victorian, Art Deco, or contemporary; or for the technique, such as cut glass, millifiore, or cameo glass. Broad keyword searches will produce pages and pages of "hits," but you're more likely to find oddly listed or incorrectly listed items that may be of interest if you use this tactic.

If you win an auction, you'll get an e-mail from eBay immediately notifying you. The seller must contact you in three days to specify the total due, including shipping and insurance, which you as winning bidder must pay. You should acknowledge this contact and respond with your confirmation of payment and shipping address. You send a check or money order (or you may pay through a credit card service like BillPoint or PayPal, if you've registered with one). When your payment is received, the seller sends the glass, boxed and insured. Glass is relatively small, light, and shippable, but scrutinize it carefully as soon as it arrives. If the seller misrepresented your item in any way, it should be returned. This can be a hassle. Unlike when you buy from a professional dealer, you have to convince the seller something is wrong, go to the trouble of mailing it back, and wait for your refund.

There is a "Feedback Forum" on eBay to weed out unscrupulous characters. Use the system—it's there to protect you. If your bid is substantial, check the seller's feedback from other purchasers before placing it. Once the transaction is completed, both seller and bidder should post brief feedback stating their satisfaction for others to see.

Live Auctions

The most important houses that hold glass auctions, or auctions that include glass, are Sotheby's, Christie's, Early's, Butterfields, David Rago, and James Julia (see page 127 for complete contact information). If you speak German, the Dorotheum in Vienna is an excellent source for glass. You won't find much American glass in Europe. The only American names known are Louis Comfort Tiffany and, more recently, Dale Chihuly.

Most authorities say new collectors should proceed with utmost caution at a live auction unless an expert is available to advise you. It is well known that dealers (and collectors) dump their mistakes in auctions. Also, there are too many ways a piece of glass can be defective or unacceptably repaired. And correct attribution is often a problem; some auction houses are extremely accurate, others are not.

You can locate auctions by reading the local newspaper, attending antiques shows, getting free trade newspapers, taking handouts from malls and shops, or subscribing to auction house catalogs. You should *always* preview an auction to check the condition of items in which you're interested. Verify that each object is actually the one advertised. Make a note of the bid number unless you have purchased a catalog beforehand. At the preview, decide on your maximum bid for each item, including the buyer's premium that most auctions charge.

When you arrive for the auction, you will fill out a bid sheet and obtain a bidder's number card to use during the auction. Always stick to your predetermined limit, no matter what. Just remember, if yours is the winning bid, you bought it, you own it.

Dealing with Dealers

Most dealers are honest and helpful. They know the key to their success lies in attracting repeat customers, and they won't get many if they lie about the merchandise or overcharge.

Let's Make a Deal

Discuss the piece that interests you with the dealer while you examine it. A pleasant inquiry, such as "Can you do any better on the price?" or "What is your best price on this?" may elicit a counter offer or discount. If this puts the item within your price range, you have a deal.

If the price is still too steep, don't ask for a further cut. Most dealers will rightly bridle if you do so after asking for their best price. And don't disparage the item! A simple "Thanks, but it's a little out of my range," provides a pleasant conclusion.

Whether you make a purchase or not, tell dealers you love their things, thank them for their time, and leave your card. You may hear from them when something else comes into their inventory. You might hear from them about the particular piece you were interested in after they think it over. Or they may stop you before you leave the booth! Dealers who have been treated with respect are much more likely to accommodate you, especially if it seems you may become a regular customer.

The first challenge for a new collector is to find dealers who are reliable and knowledgeable. A personal recommendation from another collector is the best place to start. Look for dealers who belong to a trade association with a strong code of ethics, such as the Associated Antiques Dealers of America.

Dealers should point out defects, alterations, or repairs in any glass they are selling. And many of them willingly share their encyclopedic knowledge of the subject. But you shouldn't rely on the dealer to know everything about every item—that's your job, since you're concentrating on one specialty. If you think a dealer is deliberately misrepresenting something or is simply uninformed, say thank you and walk away.

Louis Comfort
Tiffany lava
vase

Door-to-Door Collecting

A door-to-door vacuum cleaner salesman bought a Tiffany lamp from one of his customers on a whim one day. After that, he began making offers for other examples of art glass while demonstrating his cleaners in people's homes. In effect, this clever collector created his own market venue!

Eventually, this gentleman had a dazzling collection. He displayed sixteen Tiffany lamps in his living room, along with numerous étagères chock-full of art glass!

Returns and "On Approvals"

Most dealers will accept returns in as-sold condition for a good reason (for example, a piece represented as mint contains a flaw), within a reasonable amount of time (usually five to ten days of purchase or receipt), and will cheerfully refund your money. However, always examine your prospective purchase to determine if there are any chips, cracks, scratches, or flaws *before* you buy. Verify that it is what you think it is; measure for size if that is a factor; carefully check the condition of any applied decoration (gold or silver overlay, enameling, flashing). If you are satisfied with the piece after all this checking, then you are likely to enjoy it for a long time.

If you do business regularly with a dealer, you may be allowed to take a piece home *on approval,* that is, without payment. This privilege is granted if you're not sure the item will work until you get it home. You'll be obligated to pay for it or return it by an agreed-upon time, generally in one or two days. If you're fortunate enough to find a dealer who allows you to take a piece on approval, don't abuse that trust. And etiquette demands that you agree on the selling price before you take it on approval.

Sales Tax and Receipts

If a sales tax is applicable, dealers are required to collect it on your purchase.

Always get a receipt! The more expensive the item, the more details should be written down. Your receipt is your guarantee. It should include a description of the item, date made, signature or factory mark, the country where it was made, and its condition, along with the name and address of the dealer. If it's a very expensive item and you don't know the dealer, have her sign it, too. If anything is misrepresented, return it as soon as possible. It is best to examine things thoroughly before you buy, but sometimes problems aren't immediately apparent.

NOW THAT YOU'RE READY TO START COLLECTING

The Collector's Toolbox

As you begin to build your glass collection, you'll need a few tools to help you make judgments about authenticity and condition while you're out in the field.

First and foremost, your favorite reference books will help identify maker's marks and signatures. And it's extremely helpful when you can compare a potential purchase to a photo of the real thing, especially if there's a question of it being a reissue or copy. Some collectors take several price and identification guides along on a weekend buying trip.

A pocket-sized magnifying glass is an absolute *must*. You will use it constantly to check for damage and to read signatures on glass. Have a supply of soft cloths along, too. Especially at outdoor flea markets, but sometimes at indoor venues, as well, you'll need to wipe off dust and grime in order to examine a piece of glass closely.

Many experts carry a small tape measure to check diameters and heights. Ordinarily, there is a big price difference between, say, an 8" luncheon plate and a 9" dinner plate. You'll want to know exactly what you're looking at before you buy. But remember that old glassware that was handmade will almost always vary in its dimensions.

You'll want to have a supply of boxes and wrapping materials with you to protect your purchases. It's a good idea to keep them

opposite: Jeannette Glass Company Depression glass pitcher. See page 61.

in your car at all times—you never know when you'll run across an unexpected garage or estate sale.

A notepad and pen will come in handy. And many collectors carry a camera to document pieces they're considering buying or to look up more information on an unrecognized piece when they get home.

A few comments are in order about the use of ultraviolet, UV, or "black" lights in identifying glass. While some expert collectors find them indispensable, we don't advise including them in your tool kit as a beginner. So you understand what they can reveal in experienced hands, here's a quick rundown:

- A *short-wave* UV lamp will cause any lead present in glass to fluoresce, or glow, in a bluish cast. This can help identify country of origin, manufacturer, or even period in which the glass was made, depending on what you already know about the piece.

- The same *short-wave* UV lamp shown on anything purported to be Vaseline glass—a transparent yellow glass with greenish tones—will cause it to fluoresce in a yellowish cast. This glow reveals the presence of uranium in the glass, thus authenticating the piece as true Vaseline, rather than a fake.

- A *long-wave* UV lamp shown on glass in questionable condition will reveal any traces of glue used to repair it, which may be otherwise invisible to the naked eye.

Your most important tools happen to be something you can't leave by accident: your hands. You shouldn't hesitate to pick up and carefully handle (with the seller's permission, of course) any piece of glass you're seriously considering buying. Run your fingertips lightly around the rims and edges of stemware and open-form pieces to check for minor defects. Pass your fingertips over the pattern cuts in cut or engraved glass; you'll be amazed by how readily your sense of touch will reveal tiny inconsistencies in a hobnail or other decoration that signals the piece has been damaged or severely worn.

What Determines the Value of Glass?

Many factors affect values, and they may vary with the category and type of glass. All types are affected by current popularity and demand in the marketplace. Some categories tend to be more stable and others more volatile.

The price of a piece of art glass may vary by a wide margin—up or down—from one time to another, depending on market factors not related to the glass itself. A piece might be rare and fine, but if no one is collecting it, the price will remain relatively low. On the other hand, pieces of mediocre-quality, mass-produced collectible glass can soar in price if they become trendy. Remember that judging quality and judging value are two distinctly separate exercises.

Signed Steuben glass made after 1932 is one current example of exaggerated value. This glass sells at the primary-market Steuben shops for huge prices. Fair market value in the secondary market is rarely ever as high as the original purchase price, even for a piece bought many years ago. This, of course, may change in the future.

Regional differences influence prices, also. Collectors in the Midwest seem to prefer Victorian art glass, pressed glass, Carnival glass, and glass made in their own region. Big-city dwellers have a propensity for Tiffany, Lalique, cameo glass, and contemporary studio glass. Southerners have a strong preference for cut glass. A savvy collecting strategy is to specialize in something that happens to be unpopular in your area of the country. Prices are lower, and dealers may not recognize important glass that they don't usually deal in or haven't learned much about. This is often the case with contemporary signed glass. If you're looking for a price-saving niche, consider it, but don't be just a bargain hunter. First and foremost, always collect what you love, what gives you real joy.

Even with all the variables in the marketplace, there are some objective criteria that remain constant. Our experts ranked the following elements according to their impact on glass value. They reflect general guidelines, although there are no widely recognized, formal rating systems for different categories of glass.

Condition

Just as a realtor will tell you, "Location, location, location," a glass collector will tell you, "Condition is *everything!*" Glass is found for sale in every imaginable state, from pristine to deplorable. The best possible condition is *mint*. This term gets bandied about freely, but its meaning is actually quite strict. Mint means just exactly as it

Common Glass Defects

air bubbles: Inadvertent air bubbles that were in the glass when it was poured and remained after the glass cooled, or air bubbles that are the result of imperfect blowing. Sometimes glass artists add air bubbles deliberately to achieve an ornamental effect. Small air bubbles that don't detract from the appearance are not considered a major flaw by most collectors or dealers.

chip: A small piece of missing glass, usually found on the rim or foot of a piece.

cloudiness: Usually found on the inside of a vessel, a result of deposits on or etched into the glass. The most common cause is liquid that was left in the container too long. Acid in liquids such as wine or vinegar reacts with the glass. This condition may or may not be correctable, depending on severity. Pitchers, decanters, vases, cruets, and perfume bottles are most often found to be cloudy. Also called *sick glass*.

crack: A line, usually vertical, denoting damage to the glass. A crack that goes from the inside to the outside generally renders a piece worthless.

flake: A tiny missing piece of glass. Flake is used interchangeably with *fleabite*.

fleabite: See *flake*.

ground rim: A repair in which a chip on the rim of a piece was ground down to make it smooth. Usually detectable by a "sharp" feel.

Sometimes grinding throws off the proportions of a piece by interfering with its pattern, especially in cut glass.

marriage: The pairing of mismatched pieces. The two most common glass marriages are replacement stoppers in cruets, decanters, or perfume bottles, and mismatched butter dish tops and bottoms.

mold line: Seams remaining on a piece of glass where the two or three sections of the mold came together.

scratch: A mark left on glass where it came in contact with another, harder, object. The most common scratches on tableware are from serving and eating utensils. If they are slight, scratches are not considered a major defect.

strawmark: A line in glass caused by a piece of straw that was inside the mold when the glass was hot or straw that stuck to the surface of glass while it was still warm. Usually strawmarks cannot be felt with the fingers and should not be confused with scratches or cracks.

worn or blistered application: Blisters and wear damage appearing in art glass decorations such as paint, enamel, or gilding. Constant handling and/or washing are the main reasons for the damage, but extreme temperature changes can also cause it. Sometimes decorations were not fired onto art glass but were applied cold. This type of ornamentation is even more prone to wear and damage.

came from the manufacturer: no scratches, chips, stains, worn trim or decoration, or other signs of wear.

All types of glass do appear on the market in mint condition, most commonly at upscale glass or antiques shows. In other venues, it's more usual to find items in *excellent* condition, meaning they've been used but do not show heavy wear and are not chipped, scratched, or damaged. These pieces are not as expensive as those in mint condition, and will probably make up the bulk of a good collection.

A lot of the tableware you'll see will be in *used* condition, meaning that it shows signs of wear and may have chips, flakes, or nicks—but no cracks. This condition is acceptable to many collectors if the defects don't detract from the beauty or usefulness of the piece. But be wary: when a piece of glass is worn to the degree that it's obvious to the naked eye, or has visible scratches or chips, its resale value plummets.

Condition is so critical to the value of art glass that even a fleck of paint or gilding nicked on an enameled piece lessens its value. A crack renders a piece almost worthless. Only something so rare as the Portland Vase—which was smashed by a vandal at the Victoria and Albert Museum in London in 1845 and reassembled—can be excused for poor condition.

On the other hand, if you're interested in a set of glass dessert plates, you can forgive minor knife scratches, especially if you need a magnifying glass to see them. If you're going to serve food on them, you may add a few scratches of your own along the way.

Evaluating Wear and Damage

Small chips, nicks, and scratches are the most common forms of damage found on collectible glass. If the flaws are minute, they can often be polished or ground out by a professional for a minimal fee. If you're considering purchasing a damaged piece, it takes experience to judge whether the damage can be professionally repaired.

If decoration is missing on a piece with enameling or gold or silver trim, a conservator can match it perfectly.

You may find glass that has stains from liquid left in a vase or decanter. Water marks are the hardest to remove, so you'll be taking a chance if you buy such a piece (which definitely should be bargain priced). Some experts recommend allowing a mixture of vinegar and water, ammonia and water, or Lime Away and water to sit in the glass for several days. These remedies are sometimes effective, but sometimes nothing works.

Dust, dirt, grease, and oil usually can be removed on the spot with a soft cloth. Ask permission, of course, before using the cloth to buff a piece you're considering buying. Make sure that any such soil or spotting is superficial and can be removed before you buy.

Repairs and Replacements

No repairs or alterations to art glass are acceptable when it is to be sold on the open market, unless disclosed by the seller. (Pieces destined for a museum collection as examples of rare types should be repaired to make the glass more visually attractive.) It requires skill and experience to detect some kinds of damage, repairs, and alterations to art glass. Careful examination under good light with a magnifying glass is the best way to see some difficult-to-detect flaws:

- Colored glass with hairline cracks (devastating to the value of the piece)
- Pieces that have been ground down at the top, usually to eliminate a nick or chip; you can often tell by the proportions of the piece (the neck or rim may be too short) or by an interrupted pattern, unevenness, or roughness.
- A goblet or vase with a ground-down foot. The foot's roundness may be off, or it may have uneven or rough edges; anything that does not seem right is suspicious.
- Repairs to applied parts; you may see telltale traces of glue or tiny cracks.

It helps if there is a perfect example with which to compare an item that may have been damaged and repaired. This may be possible in a set of goblets or plates.

Another important reason to have reference books along when you shop is to recognize nonoriginal parts on *married* (mismatched) pieces. For instance, suppose you find a decanter you like but you suspect it doesn't have the original stopper. Many companies actually made several different styles of stoppers, so if you have your reference handy, you may discover that it is indeed the correct stopper, or that the replacement is much older (or younger) than the decanter, or that the company in question *never* made that particular stopper. If the style and fit are acceptable to you, by all means buy it, but pay 20 percent to 30 percent less for a married piece. For a decanter without a stopper, pay no more than half the price of the complete item. For art glass, any non-original element is unacceptable.

You'll find that the most commonly repaired parts of elegant glass are rims ground to remove nicks and chips and surfaces polished to remove scratches. Both of these are acceptable to most collectors and dealers so long as they do not affect pattern or color. Values for such pieces are 10 to 20 percent less than for a piece that has not been repaired. You can detect ground rims because they feel "sharp." Stemware from the factory has a perfectly smooth rim by comparison (ironically, today's glass craftsmen cannot duplicate the workmanship of fifty or seventy years ago).

Original Packaging and Labels
Original boxes and packaging for elegant glass seldom survived. It stands to reason that when consumers brought home a box of

Paperweight Series

Sulfide and floral paperweights designed in series were produced from the 1950s until the present. These are more valuable with their original boxes and certificates. As a means of authentication, however, original packaging for paperweights is not as crucial as for perfume bottles, because identifying information is usually acid stamped or engraved on the bottom of each paperweight. This documentation includes the company logo, country of origin, date, and the number of the series (for example 46/200).

Marcolin Sweden, sulphide paperweights, signed, with certificates and in their original boxes

The three twentieth-century French paperweight companies are Baccarat, St. Louis, and Cristal d'Albret. Paperweight series are made in Scotland by Perthshire and Caithness. In the United States, Paul Stankard is the leading maker of paperweight series. Stankard's weights are magnificent miniature works of art, and prices for them are quite high. Other excellent makers include the late great Charles Kasiun, the Banfords, Victor Trabucco, and Rick Ayotte.

stemware or snack sets, the first thing they did was remove the contents and discard the box (or use it to store something else). Seldom if ever will you find a complete set of tableware in its original box, but if you do, it's worth up to 25 or 30 percent more than the contents alone. One dealer reports that on the rare occasions that he finds a glass manufacturer's box, he buys it hoping to find a set of the original contents before offering it for resale.

Original boxes are exceedingly important to perfume bottle collectors. The original box and intact labels will double the price. The packaging for twentieth-century perfume bottles was very high style and an integral part of the presentation. Art Deco advertising and packaging from French glass companies, such as Lalique and Baccarat, is valuable even without the bottles!

It's unusual to find labels on tableware because even with careful washing, labels usually came off. Glass with the manufacturer's original factory label intact is worth about 20 percent more than the identical piece without the label.

Any sort of genuine identification from the manufacturer—a paper label, tag, or box—adds value to art glass. Identification is sometimes difficult because so much glass is unsigned.

Intrinsic Characteristics

Unusual design, intricate detailing, superb clarity, a particular color, or a remarkable pattern are the attributes of elegant glass that cause one example to be outstanding. These characteristics may increase the value by 25 to 50 percent compared to similar pieces.

An excellent example of unusual design is Fostoria's Quadrangle candlestick. It is a heavy, chunky-looking piece of glass with four candle arms rising from a square base. Produced in the 1930s, it was made in crystal, azure, and topaz. It is absolutely striking. Examples rarely come to market because current owners of the existing pieces likely hold onto them for their aesthetic appeal, even while they may turn over other parts of their collections for sale.

Crown is another Fostoria line that is outstanding because of its color and pattern. Produced in the 1950s and 1960s, it is a line of compotes and bowls inspired by the British Crown Jewels. Appearing shortly after the coronation of Elizabeth II, Crown was well received by the public. Without exception, each piece in this line has intricate detail, high-quality workmanship, and superb colors and design qualities—all intrinsic qualities that enhance its popularity and value.

Sometimes the detailing of a particular mold does not turn out distinctly in one pouring. In the next production run, the details are captured clearly. Discriminating collectors may pick up on this subtle nuance, valuing one example over another, even though the pieces are the same pattern, produced by the same company.

Much handmade glass has air bubbles or strawmarks; usually these don't distract from the beauty of the glass, although occasionally they do. An example with no factory flaws is highly prized.

In art glass especially, artistry, style, and the beauty of a piece make it important. Special decorating techniques, rarity, a desirable maker's signature, and perfect condition amplify the value.

Certain colors of art glass are more valuable than others. American collectors generally don't like green, orange, amber, and yellow opaque glass, preferring instead red, pink, blue, and amethyst. Demand drives up prices for the latter, while less preferred colors aren't as expensive.

Age

To be authentic, Victorian art glass should have been made in the 1880s and 1890s. If pieces in that style were made fifty years later, they are copies. Art Nouveau glass was made from the late 1880s in France until the early twentieth century in the United States. Later pieces are reproductions. The 1970s renditions of Art Nouveau are called Neo Nouveau. Each style peaks in a certain span of years. It doesn't matter how old a piece is, so long as the style is consistent with the time it should have been made. Copies are never as valuable as cutting-edge new designs.

You can date pieces by noting style, form, colors used, wear on the bottom of the glass, and signatures, and by referring to photographs in reliable published references. Your experience in handling and examining other similar pieces will be invaluable in helping you date glass accurately.

Older pieces of elegant glass are not necessarily more valuable to collectors. If a piece was poorly designed, unattractive, or inappropriate seventy years ago, it is still undesirable today. Age alone does not increase its value.

It is, however, important to be able to date elegant glass in order to authenticate it. A maker's mark stamped on the bottom provides definite identification, and sometimes will help you date it as well. For instance, Fenton Glass Company began embossing its name on the bottom of its glass in 1970. So any piece that bears no name that you can identify by pattern or other means as Fenton can be dated to the pre-1970 period. Likewise, if you've studied *Colors in Cambridge Glass,* published by the National Cambridge Collectors, you'll know what years particular colors were in production and can use color as a means of dating glass. In yet another example, Fostoria stamped its name on stemware in the 1950s, but used different labels during several production eras. If you have your reference books along, you can date a piece pretty accurately when you find a brown, yellow, or blue label.

Original manufacturer's catalogs are often reprinted by collector's clubs or national societies. They provide your best way to date glass accurately today. Be leery of dealers' claims, as their estimates of production periods are usually educated guesses, unless they've documented their research.

Rarity

Rarity in elegant glass is usually a result of the company having produced relatively little of a particular line either because it was not popular or because it was technically difficult for some reason. Molds sometimes had features that made it difficult to remove glass. For instance, Fostoria produced a rooster in crystal, black glass, and white milk glass. Due perhaps to the chemistry of the different colors, the milk glass rooster broke more frequently coming out of the mold than the black or crystal rooster. The crystal and black ones survived in considerable quantity, but few of the milk glass versions even made it to market, and they are much more valuable today for their scarcity.

Never believe someone else's claims of rarity. Expert collectors rely on published reference books and catalog reprints from specialized clubs. If you've thoroughly researched your specialty and you do find a genuinely rare example, it will probably be worth up to twice as much as similar items that are in significant supply. If a dealer claims to have researched the piece, do your own homework and check the sources cited before jumping to buy.

To determine rarity of art glass, look through major recent auction catalogs. Always crosscheck the information through reliable books and other expert collectors.

Attribution

Identifying the manufacturer of mass-produced pattern glass or cut glass is certainly an important criterion to establishing value for most collectors. Once you've researched the maker; the production details, including the years the glass was made, the colors, the number of pieces in the pattern; and the forms, you've started to build the knowledge base that will help you identify unmarked pieces. Your biggest challenge is learning to spot reproductions, whether authorized or unauthorized.

Determining attribution in art glass gets more complex. A piece is more valuable when it is signed. If a factory was known to sign pieces, an unsigned piece from that factory is less valuable, even if authenticated. A fake signature, even on a genuine piece, is bad. On the other hand, if you know the factory didn't sign its glass, the lack of a signature does not adversely affect the price. For example, the New England Glass Company did not mark its art glass. After the company moved to Ohio and its name changed to Libbey, some art glass was signed. The Mt. Washington Glass Company did sign some of its opaque art glass lines, and a signed piece is worth more than an unsigned one.

All art prices, whether fine art or decorative art, depend a lot on attribution and authentic signatures. Unfortunately, fake signatures are extremely common among the highest-priced names in art glass—Tiffany, Gallé, Lalique, and others. Examine art glass carefully to determine attribution. Look at the shape, style, and decoration. Check the bottom of the piece—that's where glass is usually (but not always) signed. You can also judge age and method of manufacture from the kind of *pontil,* or lack of it. The pontil is the place on the bottom where the glass was broken off from the blowpipe. It may be rough, left just the way it came off the blowpipe, which was the traditional Venetian method. It may be polished off in the French and English method. Traditional Bohemian glass was made without a pontil. Today's studio artists in every country make polished pontils.

Learn to identify manufacturer's marks. Heisey marked its work with a distinctive stylized *H* inside a diamond.

Who's Who in Art Glass

Here are a few of the notable designers and manufacturers whose work is highly sought. The work of some was described in detail in "Essential Background for Glass Collectors," and there are many other fine artists all over the world whose work is in great demand.

Besides Tiffany and Steuben, in *American art glass* look for Durand, Quezel, Libbey, and Nash.

In *British glass*, in addition to Thomas Webb and Stevens & Williams, look for Northwood, Hodgetts, Richardson, Walsh Walsh, James Powell & Sons, and Whitefriars.

In *French glass*, besides Gallé, Daum, and Lalique, important names are Schneider, Muller Frères, Décorchemont, Baccarat, St. Louis, and Sabino.

In *Italian glass*, in addition to Venini, Salviati, and Barovier, look for Seguso, Cenedese, Vistosi, Pauley & Cie. Outstanding contemporary artists include Lino Tagliapietra, Pino Signoretto, and Ohiro (a Japanese artist working in Murano). The American artist Robert Willson also makes his glass in Murano.

In *Bohemian glass*, besides Loetz, Moser, and Harrach, important makers were Meyers Neffe, Kralik, Palme-Konig, Riedel, and others. Contemporary studio artists are Libensky and Brychtova, Rybak, Hlava, Novak (Senior and Junior), Visner, Cerny, and Liskova.

In *Finland*, important glass designers include Aalto, Wirkkala, Sarpeneva, Tynell, Still, Nyman, and Toilkka. Almost any piece of Finnish glass with an artist's signature is collectible.

In *Sweden*, besides Gate, Hald, Lindstrand, and B. Vallien, look for A. Warff, G. Warff, Ulrica Hydman Vallien, E. Englund, S. Palmquist, E. Ohrstrom, and K. Engman. If there is an artist's name and company signed on the bottom of Swedish glass, it is collectible.

Nearly every country in Europe has splendid glass artists. There is also a strong studio glass movement in Japan, as well as fine factories such as Hoya, which makes clear glass in the Steuben/Daum/Orrefors mode.

With growing experience, you can also judge authenticity by the weight of the piece or the texture of the glass's surface. This skill comes from handling and seeing genuine pieces, so remember to hold and feel (gently!) as many pieces as possible.

Provenance

Provenance often impacts *price,* rather than value. If a well-known celebrity auctions off glass, it will likely realize prices far beyond its real value. Not many serious glass collectors consider the identity of a previous owner to be an important criterion of their collections; even fewer want to bid against avid fans of a celebrity. However, if a piece of studio glass is documented as having been part of the estate or personal collection of its designer (or of the designer's close family members), the value in glass collectors' eyes will be amplified.

If you're considering buying a piece (or pieces) of glass based on the fame of its previous owner, you should receive written documentation, signed by the seller and at least one previous owner. A thorough and detailed description of the item, the name of the maker, and place and date of its manufacture must be included. It should also be in writing that, if the provenance claim is ever proved false, the piece can be returned for a full refund. Keep any published material, such as an auction catalog, that states the particulars of prior ownership in detail.

How to Tell the Real Thing from a Reproduction, Reissue, or Fake

It seems that whenever a collectible of any kind gains enough popularity to command high prices, someone will find a way to reproduce or copy it. The creator of a knockoff may sell it with a tag identifying it as a copy, but unscrupulous dealers or collectors often remove such tags and try to palm off the new pieces as old ones to the unsuspecting. It takes an alert and sharp eye to catch these fakes. The best defense is to examine and handle authentic glass so you recognize the difference, and to buy only from reputable dealers.

Always remember this: if it seems too good to be true, it probably is. If you're offered a "rare" piece for a bargain price, especially by a dealer unknown to you whose booth contains other "rare" pieces at seemingly bargain prices, back away and take your business elsewhere.

Know your subject. Keep reference books close at hand. If you're hoping to own a rare piece someday, study examples in a museum or in other collections. Educate your eyes and hands as well as your brain. A trained eye can see minute differences in scale, and your hands will come to discern the differences in weight and surface feeling between original pieces and knockoffs. It does not happen overnight, but comes from careful study of workmanship, technique, and the details of design execution.

Probably the most conspicuous example of glass reproduction in recent years is Dalzell-Viking Glass Company's reproductions of Fostoria's popular American pattern. The reproduction pieces, made until 1998, are not marked in any way to differentiate them from Fostoria's originals of earlier years. Dalzell-Viking had workers who had been employees of Fostoria before it closed in 1986, and the company also had many of Fostoria's original molds. This was very common as glass companies often merged, were sold, or closed and sold off their assets. In trying to identify the Dalzell-Viking reproductions, visual examination may not be enough; you have to be familiar with the companies' respective histories to know that the reproductions even occurred. One of the best sources of information for this kind of "inside" historical knowledge is, again, collector's clubs. Most do a wonderful job of alerting their members in newsletters and on Web sites of reproductions, reissues, and fakes in the marketplace.

A *reproduction* uses an original mold to produce new glass with the same exact details, color, shape, and mark as the original. A *reissue* is the use of an old mold to produce glass in different colors, or with variations, or signed by the new manufacturer. In contrast to reproductions and outright fakes (copies), manufacturers' reissues of old pieces can be a wonderful thing to collect. Dealers who carry the old originals may not think so because the *restrikes* (pieces made from the original molds and materials that match the originals) may diffuse demand for the original productions they're selling. But for the collector, the reissues can be of great interest. You get an exact duplicate of the old piece, made of the same materials with the same molds, and in perfect condition because it's brand new, yet distinctly colored and/or marked with its own authentication.

If you are in doubt about the identity or authenticity of an expensive piece, get an expert opinion. Curators and other collectors in your club may be able to help, or you can pay an appraiser to thoroughly research and evaluate the piece for you. The combination of a thorough knowledge of your glass specialty, a well-trained eye, and a detailed receipt should go far to protect you from fakes, forgeries, and reproductions.

The "Business" of Collecting

There are some keys to protecting your glass collection that will pay dividends many times over. Unless you amass a huge and extremely valuable collection, the record keeping and insurance chores won't take much of your time.

Maintaining Good Records

Save your receipts. One good idea is to staple the dealer's business card to the receipt. For online transactions, you should save all e-mail between you and the seller. While it may be difficult to get a receipt from many sellers on the Web, be sure to save credit card statements, print out e-mail correspondence, and always request a detailed receipt.

Fenton Mongolian basket, c. 1935. *Courtesy of Collector's Showcase.*

Keeping track of people who sell to you is helpful for many reasons:

- You can contact the dealer if there is a problem with the merchandise.
- You can inquire about whether the dealer has any other similar pieces for you. You may want to do additional business with the dealer, perhaps to sell back something in order to buy a better piece.

97

- You can supply the dealer with your "want list." It's a good idea to have copies to give out to dealers at shows. Keep the list updated—you don't want dealers calling you about pieces you acquired long ago.
- You may need to refer to a receipt if you can't remember what you paid for the item or you need to document its value, perhaps to insure or resell the piece.
- You may want to refer to the records of your dealings with a particular seller in order to establish what kind of discount to expect.
- You may want to ask a dealer to appraise something for you.
- You may want to recommend a particularly good or helpful dealer to other collectors, especially beginners.

Making an Inventory

Keeping an inventory should be simple. There are a number of software programs designed for inventory management. Some collectors use a spreadsheet with a column for each important record.

If you prefer to keep a written record, make photocopies of the form provided here. (You may make as many copies as you need for personal use, but it is a violation of copyright to sell or distribute them to others.) Complete a form for each new addition to your collection.

Photographic records of your glass are a must. Take photographs of individual pieces for detail. Lighting glass properly for photography is difficult. Make sure you have a tripod, a black background, and paper towels or tissue paper to put over the lights. Otherwise, the reflections off the glass will ruin every picture. You can record all the pertinent information on the back of each photo, and there's your inventory system!

Use a video camera to document your collection *in the rooms where it is located.* This is very important for a valuable collection. If you don't have a video camera, rent one. Video documenting doesn't take long, and you don't need close detail. Be sure to date the videotape. You should redo this visual documentation at least once a year if you are still buying, trading, or selling.

Inventory Record

Date of purchase: _____

Purchase price: _____

Description (what the piece is): Shape, motif, color, size:

_____

Decorative techniques (e.g., engraving, enameling, gold trim):

_____

Artist or manufacturer, country of origin, signature, age (and how these details were determined):

_____

Condition (e.g., mint, excellent, good, worn, needs repair):

_____

Comments (signed? provenance? last published price?):

_____

Where purchased: _____

Address of seller: _____

Telephone/fax of seller: _____

Getting an Appraisal

An official appraisal is a thoroughly researched, written, and certified evaluation of an item or collection. It must include the reason for the appraisal (different reasons call for different methods of valuation); a complete description of the item, including photos; the method of research used; the resources consulted; the method of valuation used; and the market for which it is being evaluated.

Not many collectors invest in an appraisal just to satisfy their curiosity or to ascertain whether their glass is appreciating satisfactorily. However, an appraisal may be warranted if you want to insure a collection, sell it, or donate it to a charity for the tax write-off. It could also be useful in dividing your collection among your heirs. Sometimes a collection must be appraised as part of a divorce settlement or other lawsuit.

The appraiser must know your reason for getting an appraisal, because the reason can affect the method of valuation used. For instance, glass being appraised for insurance purposes is valued at *replacement cost*. The highest price achieved at an auction or glass show can be used to establish this value, accompanied by proper documentation. In the past, this policy of "highest possible price" was widely used by people donating glass to museums or charity, because the tax benefits were advantageous to the donor. The Internal Revenue Service has changed the rules on this issue several times, and now accepts *fair market valuation*. All such write-offs are closely scrutinized. An improper appraisal can bring big penalties, both for the person donating the glass and for the appraiser.

Appraisal at *fair market value* establishes what you can expect to receive for an item sold at current market price. It doesn't matter what you originally paid. The price must be documented, but may come from a variety of sources. Gallery prices for studio work are so high that it takes years—even in inflationary times—for the fair market price to catch up.

You want to find an appraiser who specializes in a specific area of antique and collectible glass. There are cut glass experts, pattern glass experts, Early American blown-glass specialists, and so forth—none of whom may know anything about European art glass. Ask a lot of questions before you proceed.

The best way to locate a qualified appraiser is by referral from one of the national appraisal societies. They will be able to recommend a local person with experience in the type of glass you have.

Since there are no licenses for appraisers of personal property, look for a member of the International Society of Appraisers or the American Society of Appraisers. Members of these organizations have taken accredited courses on moral and legal regulations. Ask to see credentials.

Do not hire any appraiser who charges a percentage of the appraised value of your collection. An honest and ethical appraiser will never charge that way. Also, *never* hire anyone who wants first crack at your collection if you sell. It is absolutely unethical for an appraiser to evaluate anything in which he has an interest, or to offer to buy anything she has appraised. There is one exception: some auction houses provide an expert appraisal at no charge, but they only do this if they think you have very valuable items that you will consign to the auction house for sale.

Remember that an appraisal is a document admissible as evidence in a court of law. Everything in that document should be laid out clearly, including the names of any experts the appraiser may have consulted during its preparation. It is also a confidential document. Appraisers are bound by the same client-professional privilege as attorneys and doctors, so they cannot give out any information about you or your collection. Copies of the appraisal may be forwarded to other people only upon your written request.

Expect the appraiser to require you to sign a contract. The contract should be specific, with a completion date for the report and a detailed description of the services to be provided. The fee should be specified in the contract, as well as a payment schedule (usually 50 percent upon signing the contract, with the balance to be paid upon the delivery of the report).

Remember that the appraiser must spend long hours doing research and writing your report and will expect compensation. It's possible for the appraisal fee to be higher than the value of your collection. That is why an ethical appraiser will tell you whether it makes sense for you to order the appraisal. Only you can judge whether it is worthwhile to proceed.

Insuring a Collection

Depending on the size and value of your collection, and on where you live, you may want to insure the collection. You can attach a rider to your homeowner's policy, but this is usually expensive and may be restricted. Consult your insurance agent, because some insurance companies will recommend a "fine arts policy," especial ly if you have an expensive art glass collection. Other companies may consider elegant glass to be "ordinary household contents" unless exceptional pieces are documented and insured individually. The premium will be high, and insurance will reimburse you for full replacement value only when and if you actually find and buy a replacement.

There are companies that specialize in collectibles insurance, and several authorities recommend their policies as the best choice. They are frequently less expensive than a rider on a homeowner's policy. Collector's clubs and associations are often able to offer group rates to members—another good reason to join!

LIVING WITH YOUR COLLECTION

One of the great joys of collecting glass is that it lends itself naturally to display and admiration. Even a modest collection, when tastefully placed, can express its owner's appreciation for the historical styles, designs, colors, and workmanship of glass. And once a collection grows to command its own display cabinet or étagère, it almost invariably becomes a magnet for visitors' and friends' interest and comments. You may be surprised by the number of conversations that will begin "So what have you added to your collection since I saw it last?"

Many pieces of art glass are intended to be purely ornamental. But collectors of tableware have the option to use their collections. After all, antiques and collectibles always offer an alternative to buying new household furnishings. And while most collectors would blanch at the notion of the neighborhood kids helping themselves to lemonade from beautifully etched Cambridge goblets, they wouldn't hesitate to use the same stemware to decorate a holiday table or for some other special occasion. After all, much of this glass was mass-produced. A broken piece is always a calamity, but it can usually be replaced.

Just pick up any interior decorating or design magazine to see how imaginatively professionals use period and collectible glass to set a mood, accent a color scheme, or make a statement. It's not

opposite: Durand ginger jar, signed, decorated with the pulled feather motif, 1994

even all that unusual to see culture editors like Martha Stewart mixing and matching glassware from different sets and patterns on the same table for effect. What a natural icebreaker for guests to sit down at the table and begin to admire each other's place settings!

Glass collections can enrich their owners' lives in other ways, too. One authority says, "I'm surrounded by my beautiful art glass—everywhere except the family room, since there has to be somewhere for children to play. My collection has been a constant impetus to research. I study every article and book relating to the glass I am currently interested in, which changes depending on what I find. I have studied various twentieth-century art movements because of it and have made new collector friends by sharing information."

And collectors enjoy "playing" with their glassware, dusting and rearranging it in cabinets, changing the items on tabletops. One reports, "Nothing is as relaxing as puttering with my collection. We like to change the colors around in the living and dining rooms for seasonal displays. On several occasions, neighbors have called to ask if they could bring friends to see our 'museum'!"

This section shares some of the pleasures of owning and living with a collection. It also deals with the practical points of caring for your glass and avoiding costly mistakes that could affect its value.

Displaying Your Collection

Longtime collectors are unanimous in their opinion: You'll want to be surrounded by your glass for maximum enjoyment. Most people come up with ingenious ways to display their growing collections. One woman who owns hundreds of pieces decorates each room of her house with a different glass color scheme: red glass adorns the dining room, blue the living room, green in one bedroom, cranberry in another.

A collector's display of American Victorian art glass and Swedish mid–twentieth century art glass

Another collector who wants to state "I love glass" right away has placed a glass-front china cabinet and a brass-and-glass étagère in his large foyer, flanking the front door. Guests are greeted by a glittering display that almost never fails to elicit compliments.

Closed cabinets are the safest way to display your glass and protect it from accidental bumps. They also minimize dust and other air-borne pollutants that can dull glass. Cabinets that have both glass doors and side panels offer the best display from a variety of vantage points, and the contemporary versions usually feature lighting units—either from above, below, or both.

If your decorating interests run to using antiques or period furniture throughout your home, you may want to consider using display cabinets appropriate to the periods of glass you collect. The ubiquitous bow-front oak china cabinets that graced countless parlors and dining rooms at the turn of the last century still provide pleasing backdrops for displays of art glass, brilliant cut glass, Carnival glass, or whatever your pleasure.

Open display—whether on étagères, bookshelves, wall units, or buffet and table tops—offers a less museum-like option. In these cases, you may wish to integrate glass pieces with other décor accents—books, pottery, and porcelain; framed photographs; and other memorabilia. This style of display gives you endless opportunities to "putter" with your collection, rotating pieces and replacing them with new ones, to provide constantly changing interest.

Always keep in mind traffic patterns and potential hazards. You can never overanticipate the eventualities of a vacuum cleaner cord, an excited dog's tail, or a child's absentminded tug at the corner of a table runner sending a prized piece to the floor.

For some collectors, the sheer size of their collections becomes the resounding statement of their love of glass. One collector lined a high-ceilinged den with rows of custom-made shelves to hold her 600-plus goblets. They are her pride and joy; she and her husband admire them over coffee each day with the morning sunlight illuminating the glittering display.

Amber, green, and red goblets surround a collector's den

Built-in shelving—in the kitchen, breakfast area, or dining room—often becomes the display solution for long-time collectors. This option allows the nature of the collection to dictate the display. Narrower shelves show off goblets and stemware to best effect; plate rails and grooves in shelving provide handsome, secure display for flat items; and custom-built shelving usually can be positioned to keep collections out of harm's way.

Shelving can be made of many materials, but the best for most situations is probably tempered beveled-edge glass, especially where multiple tiers of shelving are involved with either upward or downward lighting, or both.

Glass collections find natural places in the more private areas of your home, too. A favorite piece of art glass can provide daily pleasure on your home-office desk. Vanity items, perfume bottles, and crystal candlesticks can add a romantic dimension to the bedroom. If you have another collector in the family, your glass may have to share space with dolls in the armoire, or with jewelry on chests and dressers. Some collectors include the bathroom and powder room as display spaces.

There are a number of fixtures designed for glass display. Plates and bowls often show better when placed on plate stands. Clear acrylic stands don't distract from the glass. However, wooden ones or metal wire stands are more appropriate for heavy items.

COLLECTOR'S COMPASS ™

If your glass collection is insured, the carrier may have strict rules concerning how it's displayed. Be sure your agent gives you information on the type of security required—whether your collection must be kept in locked cabinets, protected by an alarm, and so forth.

If you have valuable pieces on open display, use museum wax for extra protection. You can find this inexpensive product in the glass and china departments of most department stores. A tiny ball of museum wax, placed on the bottom of a glass piece and then pressed against the surface on which it's to be displayed, will hold it firmly in place. Just remember that you've used the wax when you pick up the glass to dust or move it. If you live in an area prone to earthquakes, get local expert advice on how to protect your glass.

The interplay of light and glass surfaces is what entrances most collectors. Indeed, lighting can make a world of difference in the impact of your display. But there are some important considerations. Prolonged exposure to *direct* sunlight may cause some glass to fade or discolor. If you choose to display your glass pieces on windowsills or window shelves, try to place them in a northern exposure out of direct sunlight. Likewise, display cabinets and shelving should be out of the line of prolonged, direct sunlight if possible. If placement is an issue, you may want to look into fitting your windows with UV film that filters out the most harmful rays.

Incandescent or fluorescent lighting can be used, though there are still some safety issues. Some contemporary display cabinets feature uplighting via fluorescent tubes positioned beneath a translucent-glass base panel. This kind of lighting can be especially effective for displaying intricately cut or engraved glass. It's less satisfactory for colored glass, because of the color-cooling effect of the fluorescent lights.

When it comes to incandescent lighting you may want to consider full-spectrum bulbs—without the yellowish cast typical of regular tungsten-filament light bulbs—that mimic natural sunlight. Halogen bulbs provide an intense white light that shows off glass brilliantly. But halogen bulbs are hot. Before you purchase a display cabinet that features halogen lights, make sure that the fixture allows heat to escape. In use, avoid placing glass in close proximity to halogen bulbs. Some types of glass are prone to an instability called *crizzling*, which is aggravated by rapid or wide fluctuations in temperature. Crizzling produces a network of fine cracks in the glass.

If you're installing custom shelving and have the opportunity to design the lighting as well, consider low-voltage, recessed "puck" lights. These lights are relatively inexpensive and unobtrusive, are safer for your glass (low heat) than conventional bulbs, and can be used easily with dimmers to change the mood of your display. Whether you are installing recessed lighting in the ceiling or in a custom soffit above your shelving, they should be wired by a qualified electrician. Low-voltage fixtures are also a good choice for retrofitting an unlighted period china cabinet.

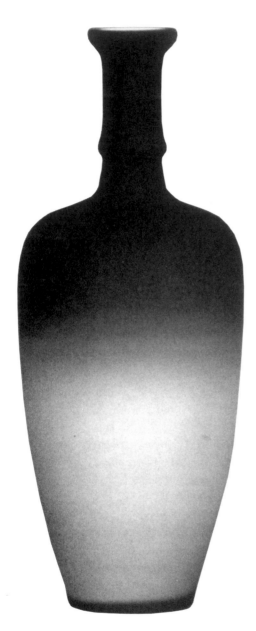

Matte finish Wheeling Peach Blow vase, the "Morgan Vase."

Caring for Your Glass

Handling and Cleaning

Art glass is a fragile and not-so-fragile collectible. Some of it is surprisingly sturdy. Pieces with sharp edges are more likely to chip than pieces that have smooth edges. Thin glass is more likely to break, even with careful handling. Lampwork is especially delicate. The less you handle fragile glass, the safer it is. Let's face it, the safest place is in a closed cabinet.

Tableware and stemware, on the other hand, were meant to be used, and there's no reason why you shouldn't. But always handle glass as if it were a piece of glass—carefully! Don't swing glass baskets by their handles. When washing stemware, be careful not to put pressure on the bowl in one direction, and on the stem the opposite way. You are apt to pop the two sections apart, as more than one collector has learned from sad experience.

There are some cardinal DON'TS to keep in mind:

NEVER put any collectible glass in a dishwasher. Cut glass will be the first to crack, since it's particularly sensitive to sudden changes in temperature. But all types of glass can easily sustain damage in a dishwasher, including chips, scratches, cracks, and abrasion marks from the detergent.

NEVER use detergents or any kind of abrasive substance on art glass that contains applied elements such as enameling, gilding, or other metallics. NEVER put these kinds of items in an ultrasonic bath either. It's actually best not to wash art glass at all, if you can avoid it. Simply dust it with a soft lint-free cloth. Tableware can be hand washed, gently, with mild dish detergent. Use a plastic basin in the sink or place a rubber mat on the bottom of the sink well for safety's sake. Don't put anything else in the sink with your glass—not even fine china—and wash each piece singly.

NEVER use anything abrasive on dry glass. If the glass surface is thoroughly wet, you can gently clean it with a plastic scouring pad without scratching it. If you are trying to remove stains from inside a decanter or vase, always dilute vinegar, ammonia, or a commercial product like Lime Away with water to create a mild solution. It's better to try longer, repeated treatments with mild remedies than strong solutions that may actually damage the glass further.

NEVER use commercial glass cleaners—the blue and green kinds—on your collectible glass. They are fine for cleaning windows, mirrors, and even the glass doors and shelves of your display cabinets—but they may contain chemicals that could be reactive with the chemicals and minerals that give your fine glass its color or finish.

Storage

If you must move your collection, or store it temporarily, always use care and common sense in packing glassware:

- Rental companies for do-it-yourself moves sell partitioned, corrugated cardboard cartons designed specifically for glassware. If these prove costly, your local liquor store may let you take some empty wine or spirits cartons, which are sturdy and contain cardboard partitions as well. If you have repeated use for them, plastic storage tubs with fitted covers may be a good option, though at substantial initial cost.
- Use tissue paper or bubble packing in sheets or bags to wrap each piece individually. Avoid the temptation to double up pieces in a single sheet of packing material. You won't be able to

remember exactly how you packed things, and one by one is invariably the best way to unpack them.

- To keep items from shifting, fill empty spaces loosely with your packing material of choice, but don't pack the cartons so tightly that you create pressure on the contents when the carton is closed and sealed.
- Don't overstack boxes filled with glassware.
- If you plan to keep your glass in storage for a prolonged period, avoid extremes of temperature and humidity. A climate-controlled storage facility is recommended, if at all possible. Garages, attics, and basements are not good storage choices if you expect to find your glass as you packed it when you take it out again.

Repairs and Restoration

In most instances, repairs become an issue because a piece of glass becomes damaged or is broken, not because you want to improve upon the "as is" condition of a piece you buy. The fact is: No repair will increase the value of a damaged or defective piece, no matter how professionally the repair was made.

Nonetheless, there are situations in which monetary value is not your first consideration. If a damaged piece has sentimental value, by all means try to have it repaired. One collector owned a rare Royal Flemish vase that had belonged to her glass teacher. It was badly cracked and she feared it would fall apart altogether; she paid handsomely to have it expertly restored. It is still worth little, if anything, on the market, although it would be very valuable in perfect condition. Was the repair worth it to her? "Absolutely," she states unequivocally.

Equally unequivocally, we can state: NEVER try to repair art glass yourself, however minor the damage.

If you want to keep a damaged piece of tableware for display only (not to use), there are a number of epoxy cements and special glass adhesives that are suitable for do-it-yourself use. The tiniest of chips or flakes in a glass's rim may be carefully smoothed out with an emery board, or better, with a sheet of superfine wet/dry emery cloth. Larger chips and flakes should be ground out with an abrasive wheel by a professional glass repairer.

Glass that's been stained by an acidic substance such as wine or plant juices may be treated at home using dilute solutions of vinegar and water, ammonia and water, commercial lime-dissolving agents and water, or even denture cleaner. None of these remedies is surefire, but used conservatively, they won't make the condition worse.

"Sick glass" is cloudiness inside the glass. Some glass repairers use a process to "tumble out" cloudiness, but you're running the risk of breakage by going this route.

It may be difficult to find a good glass repair shop. A museum curator, a trusted glass dealer, or your collector's club may be able to recommend someone. Or try *Maloney's Antiques and Collectibles Resource Directory* to locate one in your area. Otherwise, you have to deal with expensive, time-consuming, and risky shipping.

New Martinsville etched "Canterbury" Depression glass, 1932–1944. *Courtesy of Collector's Showcase.*

IF AND WHEN YOU DECIDE TO SELL PIECES FROM YOUR GLASS COLLECTION

Why You Might Want to Sell All or Parts of Your Collection

There are as many reasons to sell pieces from your collection as there are collectors themselves. Perhaps you'd like to trade up from a so-so example to a truly outstanding one. Maybe you've accumulated a number of duplicate pieces that you'd like to winnow down. Perhaps your interest in glass has waned (incredible to believe as that may be), and you'd like to explore another field of collecting. Or maybe you just need the money.

You Want to Trade Up to Better Examples

Collections are dynamic. Over time, they not only increase in scope and size, but they also change in focus. A beginning collector usually starts out on a small scale, both in terms of quantity and price. But a more experienced collector has higher expectations about the quality of the items he or she buys. As you become more confident, you'll no doubt want to trade up to more desirable, and, usually, more expensive items.

In art and studio glass, almost every designer's repertoire ranges from mediocre to fabulous pieces. If you bought less-inspired work in the beginning, you may now want to acquire the best pieces.

You've Acquired Bargain or Duplicate Pieces You No Longer Need

As you become more knowledgeable and confident as a collector, you might purchase underpriced items that aren't particularly appealing to you personally just because they're a bargain. Your motive is to make a profit by reselling them. If you hunt for glass actively, you can accumulate quite an inventory of this type of item in a short time, little of which you're probably interested in keeping as part of your permanent collection. Many collectors sell or trade duplicates or bargain pieces to secure a "crown jewel" for their collections—another reason it's important to network with others and join a collecting group.

Where to Sell Pieces from Your Collection

Local Dealers

An obvious choice is to take your cache to a local glass dealer—perhaps one with whom you regularly shop. But realize that most dealers rely on an average 100 percent markup. This means that if you'd normally see the item priced at $100 in their shop, they're not likely to pay you more than $50 for it. Is this fair? Certainly, the dealer has expenses to meet, many of which may not be obvious to the casual shopper. In addition to the cost of renting space in which to do business, the dealer has utility expenses, advertising expenses, travel expenses, and possibly payroll expenses. And last but not least, the dealer hopes to take home enough to pay him- or herself a salary.

Is a dealer's shop the best place to sell your glass? Perhaps—if you regularly expect to pick up and sell bargain items and your main goal is to turn a quick, though likely modest, profit on them. You also may build a tremendous amount of goodwill in the process: The shop owner may cut you better price breaks on items you purchase because of your regular business. He or she may also attempt to "cherry pick," making you an offer for the best pieces and leaving you with the rest. Evaluate your options carefully before moving too fast. There are still a number of other avenues to explore.

Consignment Selling

If your goal is to maximize your profit, taking whatever time is necessary, consignment selling might be a better alternative—especially if you're intent on selling locally and you have a good rapport with a specific dealer. Many shops will sell your items in their stores for a percentage of the selling price, which may range up to 50 percent. They benefit by not having to pay up front for the item to have it in inventory, and they may get to handle your highly desirable pieces as "traffic builders" with their key customers; you benefit because you might receive a higher selling price at retail, even taking the selling commission into account. Of course, if the item never sells, you receive nothing. And in some cases, you might wait for several weeks or months for the item to sell.

Live Auctions

Live auctions are different from online auctions, in that you're putting your glass in the hands of a professional auctioneer. Auctions are sometimes held in association with club shows, too. In those cases, one of the club officers may act as the auctioneer.

Your concerns beforehand are:

- Is the auctioneer reputable? He should be a member of a recognized auctioneers' association. If you have an extremely valuable collection that includes rare pieces, you should shop around until you find an auctioneer who has specific expertise in glass.
- Where does he advertise, and how effectively? The results of a live auction depend entirely on the turnout of bidders. You want a large crowd on auction day, but more important, you want individuals there who have come to bid on your glass items.
- Does the auctioneer produce a catalog? High-end auctions are generally cataloged. Each lot is photographed, described in detail, and an estimate may be given. Auctioneers who produce catalogs likely have extensive mailing lists to solicit interested collectors. The catalog may be sold individually to the public, mailed to subscribers, and/or mailed free to preferred customers.
- How will your glass be sold? If you're liquidating an art glass collection, separate it into categories. Signed, perfect pieces might go to a big auction house or into a specialized art glass auction. More ordinary, unsigned, or imperfect glass is appropriate for selling in lots at a general auction or an estate sale. The

auctioneer's job is to hammer down every lot that goes on the block. If he's not a glass expert, you need to give him guidance on how pieces should be grouped or sold individually. You should also specify any reserve prices you may want to set, though auctioneers are often resistant to reserves and would rather open the bidding at a higher level.

- What's the commission? Auctioneers usually charge a percentage on the amount of the winning bid. If you have a large collection to auction, you may be able to negotiate the commission. It never hurts to ask.

Advertising and Direct Selling

You can try placing ads in your local newspapers, general antiques weeklies such as *Antique Trader,* specialized glass papers such as *The Daze,* or in classified sections of glass-related Web sites. Newspapers tend to have the highest rates and so may not be cost-effective for less expensive items. And the market in your particular area might not be strong for the specific item you want to sell. Trade publications usually have lower ad rates, and the audience you reach is more targeted and broad-based. This usually gives you greater leverage as a seller. Web sites may be better still; they reach a broad but targeted audience, and the cost of advertising on them usually is minimal.

Your descriptive listing will be all-important, as this is generally a two-step selling process. It's also a good idea to maintain your privacy by listing only your name, a post office box address, phone number, and e-mail address in your ads. If they work, the ads will generate correspondence from people wanting to know more. Then, you've got to be ready to send a more detailed description and photo (a digital image if you're using the Internet) of the piece(s) in which potential buyers are interested. You may hear back from some of them a second time, with more questions or with an attempt to negotiate a purchase with you.

If you're selling glass on the side, mail order can be a pretty distracting way to do business. You'll get phone calls and voice-mail messages at all times of day or night, and you'll end up playing a lot of phone tag with call-backs. You've got a lot of work to do, both on the phone and at the post office, to get information to people and answer their questions. And if you're lucky and get two people interested in buying the same piece, you're faced with conducting an "auction" yourself that can easily backfire and end up in no sale.

Or, you may wonder why you're getting no calls only to learn that you missed the ad deadline, and you have to sit it out until the next issue closes. Maybe your ad didn't get good placement in the magazine and you get few calls. Most dealers who have success in this venue advertise repeatedly and set themselves up to make this a primary business.

Antiques Malls

Antiques and collectibles malls present a number of advantages. They're a kind of "long-term show" in that the people who come through their doors are largely dealers and collectors who may be looking for specific wants, or just browsing. At any given moment the traffic isn't as bustling as at a weekend show, but you capture many potentially interested "eyeballs" by displaying your glass at a mall. Depending on the mall, you may only be obliged to pay the rental fee for your space or display case plus a commission on sales. Some malls expect you to put in time there as part of your contract.

Malls are usually fairly well organized, clean, and have standard credit and discount policies. The mall employees show the items to interested customers, process credit card payments, write receipts, and wrap the purchases. You just pay the rental fee and a commission on what sells. You may also be expected to rotate your stock periodically to keep the mall's inventory looking fresh.

What could be the downside? Your merchandise can get lost among the hundreds of cases in a large mall. Malls offer general collectible merchandise, so the number of glass collectors, and the number of collectors who may find your specialty in glass appealing, may be relatively few compared with more targeted venues.

You may find that you've associated yourself with a mall that lacks upstanding policies on carrying reproductions and fakes. While your glass is original and authentic, word may be out on the mall among collectors to stay away. It pays to do a careful walk of the mall before committing to a lease, to make your own observations about the overall quality of the merchandise.

In a worst-case scenario, you may find at the end of your mall lease that you sold little or nothing. In the meantime, your investment has been sitting there. That's why seasoned dealers use different sales venues simultaneously. They may be attending shows, stocking a mall case, selling online, or even putting up pieces of glass at live auction—all simultaneously.

Online Selling

Many collectors and dealers have turned to online auctions as a means of quickly and successfully selling their pieces. You reach a much larger bidding audience, the auctions usually are over in seven to ten days, and you can set reserve prices below which you won't sell. Another benefit is that buyers sometimes get caught up in bidding wars that drive your items to final selling prices far in excess of their market value.

Today many glass collectors (and dealers) are establishing their own Web sites or leasing "cyberspace" at aggregation Web sites such as www.megashow.com. At these on-line "malls," pieces are available to a worldwide audience twenty-four hours a day, seven days a week.

How to List Your Glass for Sale

First of all, remember that the more information you can provide, the better. At the very least, list the designer (if known), the manufacturer, the pattern, the condition, and of course, the price. Also describe any repairs or difficult-to-find flaws in the item. In the long run, you'll reap more by forging a reputation as an honest seller than you'd ever gain by failing to disclose pertinent information about an item.

Online auctions are perhaps the best way for new glass collectors to sell their pieces. But you need to remember that most online auctions rely on their internal search engines to steer prospective bidders to items. For example, if a bidder happens to be looking for Heisey Lariat pattern tableware, you as the seller would be remiss to leave out the manufacturer's name (Heisey) or the pattern name (Lariat) because those are the most likely words potential buyers will search for in addition to the specific type of piece they may be seeking (for instance, covered candy dish).

Here are examples of poorly written and well-written online auction descriptions.

A Poorly Written Description

Carnival glass bowl. No chips. Plus shipping.

A Well-Written Description

Fenton Carnival Glass—Butterfly and Berry bowl 9"
diameter with scalloped edge. Bronze, green and blue
iridescent, cobalt background. 3 claw and ball feet.
Original Fenton label. Excellent condition, no
defects. Winner pays $8.00 priority shipping and
insurance within the U.S.

Of course, in a fixed-price advertisement—in any of the
media we're discussing—you'd also include your asking price.

You Want to Become a Dealer?

Many collectors who have acquired a lot of stuff eventually find
themselves considering this role. And why not? What better way is
there to make an income than by dabbling in something you're
passionate about?

But being a dealer is not as easy as printing business cards and
renting a table or booth at a show. There are many considerations,
including accumulating and storing your inventory, tagging each
item, making arrangements for shows (reserving booth space,
accommodations, travel, and so on), signing leases for space if
you're trying a mall venue, writing and placing ads—not to mention your legal obligations to state and federal taxing authorities.
You also need to be confident that you know enough about the
glass you plan to sell to go into the marketplace and hold your own
with other dealers, as well as to talk to prospective customers who
will be full of questions.

Read an introductory book about running a small business or
consult with a small-business counselor before you decide you
want to take this route. Being a dealer is a huge investment of
time—and money. Make sure you want to do this badly enough
before you get in too deep. If you decide to give it a try, there are
a number of ways you can go.

Shows

You've undoubtedly had great times attending shows as a collector. You may have had to endure the inconvenience of standing in line to get into a good show, but once inside you did your hunting, stopped when you felt like it, and most of the time, went back to the comfort of your home at the end of the day to enjoy your new treasures.

Thus, you'll probably already know which are the best shows in your area in terms of the number and quality of dealers, as well as crowd turnouts. But as a dealer, be prepared for an arduous experience. First, there's the red tape of renting booth space (which may not be easily available to newcomers or may be in the most undesirable locations). You have to pack and transport your inventory to the show site. Then there's the "load-in" and set up, which is usually either the day before the show or at the crack of dawn the day of the show. You run the risk of items being damaged in transit.

Be prepared for physical labor, long hours, and substantial cash outlay before your first customer even steps into your booth. Then once the show gets started, and if it's a good show (which is what you want), you'll be standing and talking for seemingly endless hours until closing. You'll have to watch for "light-fingered" customers who may make off with your goods. Unless you're sharing booth duties with another dealer or a buddy, you may not be able to duck away to visit the restroom or grab a quick bite when you feel like it. And when the show ends, the work of breakdown, packing, and "load-out" is still ahead.

Of course, there are no guarantees. The show may be poorly attended for any number of reasons. If you haven't made the effort to present your inventory in an attractive way—nicely arranged and well-lit—potential customers may pass you by in favor of better merchandised booths where the glass seems to sparkle a little brighter. Maybe your asking prices were off current market values, or other dealers showed up with more desirable merchandise. Perhaps you just had a lousy spot in the back of the room. Any and all of these factors can affect your outcome.

Is it worth it? If you end up with a profit after you've covered your investment in glass and all expenses door to door, consider it a great show. Then all the "fringe benefits" of hotel room hopping, buying and selling with other dealers before opening, learning

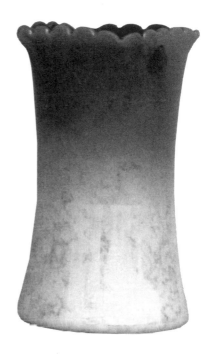

more about glass than you knew before, making new contacts, and so on, become dividends to offset all the personal time and hard work you put into the show.

New England
Glass Works
agata vases

Dealing with One of Life's Certainties

If you've been a little lax about record keeping as a collector, you can't afford to make the same mistake as a dealer—whether you're selling by mail order, online, at shows, or in malls. As a seller of any kind, you deal with state and federal taxing authorities.

Any state that imposes a sales tax will expect you to collect and pay state sales tax for any sales you make in person in that state. Your home state will expect you to collect and pay state sales tax on all sales you make to customers within the state—whether indirectly via mail-order and the Internet, or directly in person. So, if you travel to another state to do a show, be prepared to register with that state's taxing authority. Some states are more vigilant than others; it's not unusual to find state agents walking shows, randomly interviewing dealers for compliance. The show promoter will usually provide necessary information on state sales tax compliance with your exhibitor contract and materials.

The Internal Revenue Service views your glass selling as a business, however casually you may do it. Get into the habit of keeping a notebook and record your expenses on every type of sale you make, from door to door—even down to the mileage to the antiques mall to change the stock in your case. If you do a number of shows, you might want to get some manila clasp envelopes for receipts. Label and date one for each show you do, and stuff all your receipts into it as you go.

If you haven't kept a good inventory list or database of your collection before now, it's essential that you make one before you start selling. Your inventory should include—at the least—a detailed description of each item and its condition, the documented price you paid for it, and the year in which you purchased it. The IRS is interested in any profit you recognize when you sell over what you originally paid, plus the expenses of marketing. Your cost in the item, in addition to your other dealer expenses, is part of the cost of selling it. It's best to consult with your tax professional or accountant before you set out as a dealer. He or she will be able to counsel you on the details of your individual situation so that you'll be complying with the law. Your numbers person may be able to give you some pointers to help minimize the amount of tax you'll owe at the end of the year. He or she can also help you apply for a tax ID or resale number and explain why that may a good idea for you.

Donating Your Collection

You may have reasons to donate your collection to an organization or institution. Depending on your situation, it may be financially your best move, or at least one with tax advantages. Consult with your tax professional and attorney if you're considering this option and be sure you understand all the angles.

Donating your collection is a way to ensure that your collection stays together and will be well cared for following your stewardship of it. First you need to identify the institution. It may be a local museum, a library, a historical society, or other qualified nonprofit, tax-exempt organization.

Make sure the institution wants the collection, is prepared to care for it, and has a plan to exhibit it (at least initially). Work out all the details in writing before you make a commitment—what credit you'll receive, how the collection will be conserved and displayed, and whether it can ever be sold.

You may have to get the collection appraised if you're expecting a tax deduction, and of course, your gift must be to a qualified nonprofit entity. Your tax professional will be able to guide you through the tax compliance details relating to gifts of property.

Most important, make sure you're emotionally ready to part with your collection. You can visit your former collection in its new home, but once donated, you can't take your glass back.

Vienna Secession
glass, design
attributed to
Joseph Hofmann,
unsigned, c. 1914

RESOURCES TO FURTHER YOUR COLLECTING

Shows

Atlantique City
P.O. Box 1800
Ocean City, NJ 08226
Brimfield Associates
(800) 526-2724
www.atlantiquecity.com

Continental Shows, Ltd.
P.O. Box 843
Burnet, TX 78911
(512) 756-9731
General antiques show, excellent from a glass buyer's standpoint. Wonderful promoter to work with from dealer's standpoint. Highly recommended.

Farmington Antiques Weekend
Farmington, CT
Revival Promotions
P.O. Box 388
Grafton, MA 01519
(508) 839-9735
www.farmington-antiques.com

Fostoria Glass Society of America Annual Show and Sale
P.O. Box 826
Moundsville, WV 26041
Held annually during the second week of June in conjunction with the Fostoria convention in Moundsville.

Gaithersburg Antique & Collectible Show

Montgomery County
Fairgrounds
Gaithersburg, MD 20877
(301) 216-0876
February, May, and October annually. All kinds of glass books, including out-of-print.

National Depression Glass Association Show and Sale

P.O. Box 8264
Wichita, KS 67208-0264
Held annually in conjunction with the association's convention during the second weekend of July. Location varies.

Sanlando Depression Era Glass Show and Sale

Millie Downey
P.O. Box 560275
Orlando, FL 32856-0275
(407) 298-3355
Annual January show at Sanford Civic Center, Sanford, Florida.

Washburn's San Antonio Glass Show

Kent Washburn
8048 Midcrown, Suite 26
San Antonio, TX 78218-2334
(210) 599-0635
washburnk@aol.com
Held annually, second week of February. The best show in the Southwest for rare and unusual examples of American-made elegant and Depression glassware.

Galleries Specializing in Contemporary Studio Glass

Berengo Art Galleries

Fondamenta Vetrai 109/a
30141 Murano
Venezia, Italy
+39.41.739453

Kortestraat, 7
6811 EN Arnhem
The Netherlands
+31.26.3518477
www.berengo.com

Collector's Showcase

Star Center Mall
829 2nd St.
Snohomish, WA 98290
(360) 568-1339

The Glass Gallery

4720 Hampden Lane
Bethesda, MD 20814
voice/fax: (301) 657-3478
www.artline.com/galleries/glass/glass.html

Habatat Galleries

608 Banyan Trail
Boca Raton, FL 33431
(561) 241-4544

7 Saginaw St.
Pontiac, MI 48342
(248) 333-2060
www.habatat.com

The Heller Gallery
420 W. 14th St.
New York, NY 10014
(212) 414-4014

Maurine Littleton Gallery
1667 Wisconsin Ave. NW
Washington, DC 20007
(202) 333-9307

Auction Houses Dealing in Glass

Butterfields (an eBay company)
220 San Bruno Avenue
San Francisco, CA 94103
(415) 861-7500

7601 Sunset Blvd.
Los Angeles, CA 90046
(323) 850-7500

441 West Huron
Chicago, IL 60610
(312) 377-7500
www.butterfields.com

Christie's
Rockefeller Center
20 Rockefeller Plaza
New York, NY 10020
(212) 636-2000

219 East 67th St.
New York, NY 10021
(212) 606-0400

360 North Camden Drive
Beverly Hills, CA 90210
(310) 385-2600
www.christies.com
The Christie's Web site lists its sales offices and auction houses worldwide.

Craftsman Auctions
1485 W. Housatonic
Pittsfield, MA 02101
(413) 448-8922
www.artsncrafts.com

William Doyle Galleries
175 East 87th St.
New York, NY 10128
(212) 427-2730
www.doylenewyork.com

Early's Auction Company
123 Main St.
Milford, OH 45150
(513) 831-4833

ewolfs.com
1239 West 6th
Cleveland, Ohio 44113
(800) 526-1991
www.ewolfs.com
An exclusively online auction that features fine art glass among its other decorative art offerings plus the occasional all-glass auction (most recently December 1999). Also maintains a fixed-price, direct-purchase gallery that includes European and American glass.

James D. Julia Auctioneers, Inc.
Route 201 Skowhegan Rd.
P.O. Box 830
Fairfield, ME 04937
(207) 453-7125
www.juliaauctions.com

Pacific Glass Auctions
1507 21st St., Suite 203
Sacramento, CA 95814
(916) 443-3296
www.pacglass.com

Palais Dorotheum Vienna
Dorotheergasse 17
A-1010 Vienna
Austria
+431-51560-0

David Rago Auctions, Inc.
333 N. Main St.
Lambertville, NJ 08530
(609) 397-9374
www.ragoarts.com/nj

Rose Galleries
2717 Lincoln Drive
Roseville, MN 55113
(888) 484-1415
www.rosegalleries.com

Skinner
The Heritage on the Garden
63 Park Plaza
Boston, MA 02116
(617) 350-5400
www.skinnerinc.com

C.G. Sloan and Company
4920 Wyaconda Road
Rockville, MD 20852
(800) 649-5066

Sotheby's
1334 York Ave.
New York, NY 10021
(212) 606-7000
www.sothebys.com

Sotheby's Beverly Hills
9665 Wilshire Blvd.
Beverly Hills, CA 90212
(310) 274-0340
www.sothebys.com

Sotheby's Chicago
215 West Ohio St.
Chicago, IL 60610
(312) 396-9599

John Toomey Gallery
818 North Blvd.
Oak Park, IL 60301
(708) 383-5234
www.treadwaygallery.com

Treadway Gallery Incorporated
2029 Madison Road
Cincinnati, OH 45208
(513) 321-6742
www.treadwaygallery.com

Weschler's
909 E St. NW
Washington, DC 20004
(800) 331-1430
www.weschlers.com

Wright
1140 West Fulton
Chicago, IL 60607
(312) 563-0020
www.wright20.com
Although Wright deals primarily in Mid-Century Modern furniture, you can also find glass of the same era here.

Publications

In addition to the general publications listed here, remember that virtually every one of the dozens of collectors' clubs and societies publishes a newsletter on its specific area of glass collecting.

Antique Trader Weekly
P.O. Box 1050
Dubuque, IA 52004-1050
(800) 334 7165
www.collect.com/antiquetrader

The Daze
P.O. Box 57
Otisville, MI 48463
(810) 564-4011
www.dgdaze.com

Glass Quarterly
UrbanGlass
647 Fulton Street
Brooklyn, NY 11217-1112
(718) 625-3685
www.urbanglass.com

Glass Art Society Journal
1305 Fourth Ave, Ste. 711
Seattle, WA 98101-2401
www.glassart.org

Glass Collector's Digest
Antique Publications
P.O. Box 553
Marietta, OH 45750-0553
(800) 533-3433
www.antiquepublications.com

Maine Antique Digest
P.O. Box 1429
Waldoboro, ME 04572
(207) 832-7534
www.maineantiquedigest.com

Neues Glas/New Glass
GLP International
153 S. Dean Street
Englewood, NJ 07631
(201) 871-1010
www.glpnews.com
Quarterly featuring contemporary glass; published in German and English.

New Glass Review
Corning Museum of Glass
One Museum Way
Corning, NY 14830-2253
(607) 937-5371
www.cmog.org

Collector's Clubs and Associations

The listings here will put you in touch with the national groups in major collecting categories. Many of these groups (and others) have regional, state, and local branches. And there are many more clubs devoted to very specific categories of glass.

American Carnival Glass Association
9621 Springwater Lane
Miamisburg, OH 45342

American Cut Glass Association, Inc.
P.O. Box 482
Ramona, CA 92065-0482
www.cutglass.org

Collectors of Crackle Glass Club
P.O. Box 1186
Massapequa, NY 11758
(516) 799-2619

Early American Glass Traders
RD 5, Box 638
Milford, DE 19963

Early American Pattern Glass Society
P.O. Box 266
Colesburg, IA 52035
(319) 856-2025

Fenton Art Glass Collectors of America
P.O. Box 384
Williamstown, WV 26187
(304) 375-6196

Fostoria Glass Collectors, Inc.
P.O. Box 1625
Orange, CA 92856
www.fostoriacollectors.org

Fostoria Glass Society of America
P.O. Box 826
Moundsville, WV 26041

Glass Research Society of New Jersey
Wheaton Village
Millville, NJ 08332

Heisey Collectors of America
National Heisey Glass Museum
169 West Church St.
Newark, OH 43055
(740) 345-2932
heiseymuseum.org/hca

International Paperweight Society
123 Locust St.
Santa Cruz, CA 95060
(800) 538-0766
www.paperweight.com

International Perfume Bottle Association
396 Croton Road
Wayne, PA 19087
(610) 995-9051
www.perfumebottles.org

Lalique Collectors Society
400 Veterans Blvd.
Carlstadt, NJ 07072
(800) 274-7825
www.lalique.com

Mt. Washington Art Glass Society
P.O. Box 24094
Fort Worth, TX 76124-1094

The National American Glass Club
P.O. Box 8489-W
Silver Spring, MD 20907-8489
*Members study new and old glass
from all over the world. Seminars,
library collections, trips, publications.
The Glass Club Bulletin and Glass
Shards. Some chapters publish local
newsletters.*

National Cambridge Collectors, Inc.
P.O. Box 416
Cambridge, OH 43725-0416
www.cambridgeglass.org

National Capital Heisey Collectors
P.O. Box 23
Clinton, MD 20735

National Depression Glass Association
P.O. Box 8264
Wichita, KS 67208-0264

National Fenton Glass Society
P.O. Box 4008
Marietta, OH 45750
www.axces.com/nfgs

**National Imperial Glass Collector's
Society**
P.O. Box 534
Bellaire, OH 43906

**Old Morgantown Glass Collectors
Guild**
P.O. Box 894
Morgantown, WV 26507-0894

Tiffin Glass Collectors Club
P.O. Box 554
Tiffin, OH 44883

Museums

United States

American Craft Meuseum
40 W. 53rd St.
New York, NY 10019
(212) 956-3535

Bennington Museum
West Main Street
Bennington, VT 05201
(802) 447-1571

Cambridge Glass Museum
P.O. Box 416
Cambridge, OH 43725-0416
(740) 432-4245
www.cambridgeglass.org
*A new museum is under construction;
the old one was destroyed by flood. The
collection is temporarily housed at the
Penny Court Antiques Mall in down-
town Cambridge.*

Carnegie Institute Museum of Art
4400 Forbes Ave.
Pittsburgh, PA 15213-4080
(412) 622-3131
www.cmoa.org

Chrysler Museum of Art
245 West Olney Rd.
Norfolk, VI 23510-1587
(757) 664-6200
helios.whro.org/cl/cmhh

Corning Museum of Glass
One Museum Way
Corning, NY 14830-2253
(607) 937-5371
www.cmog.org
In addition to superb glass exhibits,
including many antiquities, Corning
has the best glass library in the country
and a center on the science of glass-
making.

Fostoria Glass Society of America
Museum
Sixth Street at Tomlinson Avenue
P.O. Box 826
Moundsville, WV 26041
(304) 845-9188
www.fostoriaglass.org

Henry Ford Museum
20900 Oakwood Blvd.
Dearborn, MI 48124-4088
(313) 271-1620
www.hfmgv.org

High Museum of Art
1280 Peachtree St. NE
Atlanta, GA 30309
(404) 733-4400
www.high.org

Historical Glass Museum Foundation
1157 Orange St.
P.O. Box 921
Redlands, CA 92373
(909) 798-0868
www.rth.org/lookingglass

Huntington Galleries
Park Hills
Huntington, WV 25701
(304) 529-2701

Jones Museum of Ceramics
and Glass
35 Douglas Mountain Road
Sebago, ME 04029
(207) 787-3370

Metropolitan Museum of Art
1000 Fifth Avenue
New York, NY 10028-0198
(212) 535-7710
www.metmuseum.org

Mills Collection of American Pressed
Glass
Reed Hall
Texas Christian University
2800 S. University Drive
Fort Worth, TX 76129
(817) 257-7000
www.tcu.edu

Morse Museum of American Art
445 North Park Avenue
Winter Park, FL 32789
(407) 645-5311
www.morsemuseum.org

Museum of American Glass at
Wheaton Village
1501 Glasstown Road
Millville, NJ 08332-1566
(800) 998-4552
www.wheatonvillage.org

The Museum of Modern Art
    11 West 53rd Street
    New York, NY 10019
    (212) 708-9400
    www.moma.org

National Heisey Glass Museum
    169 West Church Street
    Newark, OH 43055
    (740) 345-2932
    www.heiseymuseum.org

National Museum of American History
    Smithsonian Institution
    14th St. and Constitution Ave. NW
    Washington, DC 20560
    (202) 357-2700
    americanhistory.si.edu

Oglebay Institute Glass Musuem
    Carriage House in Oglebay Park
    two mi. N. of I-70 on Rt.88
    Wheeling, WV 26003
    (800) 624-6988
    Offers glass blowing and decorating demonstrations, as well as the display of an extensive collection of antique to modern glass. The park is also home to the West Virginia Glass and Crafts Festival in late July and early August.

Renwick Gallery
    National Museum of American Art
    The Smithsonian Institution
    Pennsylvania Avenue at 17th Street, N.W.
    Washington, D.C.
    (202) 357-2700

Bill and Irma Runyon Art Collections
    Forsyth Center Gallery
    Memorial Student Center
    Joe Routt Blvd. and Clark Street
    Texas A&M University
    College Station, TX 77843
    e-mail: forsyth@msc.tamu.edu
    One of the world's most extraordinary collections of English Cameo Glass, as well as 1,100 American and English glass objects. The Glass Collections include the mastery of Louis Comfort Tiffany, Steuben Glass Works, Mount Washington Glass Company, New England Glass Company, and long-term loans of Gallé and rich-cut glass

Toledo Museum of Art
    2445 Monroe Street
    Toledo, OH 43620
    (800) 644-6862
    www.toledomuseum.org

William Benton Museum of Art
    University of Connecticut
    245 Glenbrook Rd. U-140
    Storrs, CT 06269-2140
    (860) 486-4520
    www.benton.uconn.edu

Europe
Broadfield House Museum
    Compton Drive
    Kingswinford
    West Midlands
    DY6 9NS
    England
    +44 (0) 1384-812-745
    www.dudley.gov.uk

Decorative Arts Museum
Musée des Art Decoratifs
Palais du Louvre
107, rue de Rivoli
75001
Paris, France
+44 55 57 50
www.paris.org/Musees/Decoratif
s/info.html

Finnisches Glasmuseum
Tehtaankatu 23
Fin-11910
Riihimäki
Finland
+358 (0) 19741-7494
www.riihimaki.fi/lasimus/

Glasmuseum
Strandvejan 8
DK-8400 Ebeltoft
Denmark
+45-8634-1799
glasmuseet@glasmuseet.dk

Glass Art Museum
Passaur Glasmuseum
Am Rathausplatz
94032
Passau, Germany
+49 0851-35071
www.passau.de/passau/Kutur/gla
smuse.htm

Glass Museum
Sklárské Muzeum
C2-473 01
Nový Bor, Nám Míru 105
Czech Republic
+42 424 321 96
www.gallery.uunet.be/Loetzweb/
museums/htm

Kunstmuseum Düsseldorf
Ehrenhof 5, D-40479
Düsseldorf, Germany
+49-211-89-92460
kunstmuseum_duesseldorf@
compuserve.com

Smålands Museum (Swedish Glass Museum)
Södra Järnvägsgatan 2
Box 102
SE-351 04 Växjö
Sweden
0470-451-45
www.smalandsmuseum.g.se

Victoria and Albert Museum
Cromwell Road
South Kensington
London, England SW7 2RL
+44(0)20 7942 2000
www.vam.ac.uk

For access to a wide rage of information on museums, galleries, clubs, and other Web sites pertaining to collectible glass, go to www.glass.co.nz/links.htm.

BIBLIOGRAPHY AND RECOMMENDED READING

Elegant, Pattern, and Depression Glass

Archer, Margaret, and Douglas Archer. *Imperial Glass*. Collector Books, 1978.

Avila, George C. *The Pairpoint Glass Story.* Reynolds-DeWalt, 1968.

Ball, Joanne D., and Dorothy H. Torem. *Commercial Fragrance Bottles*. Schiffer, 1993.

Bones, Frances. *Fostoria Glassware, 1887–1982*. Collector Books, 1999.

Bordignon, Carla. *Perfume Bottles*. Chronicle Books, 1995.

Bredehoft, Neila. *Collector's Encyclopedia of Heisey Glass, 1925–1938*. Collector Books, 1986. Values updated 1999.

Bredehoft, Tom, and Neila M. Bredehoft. *Fifty Years of Collectible Glass, 1920–1970*. Antique Trader Books, 2000.

—. *Hobbs, Brockunier & Co. Glass: Identification and Value Guide*. Collector Books, 1997.

Edwards, Bill, and Mike Carwile. *Standard Encyclopedia of Carnival Glass,* 6th ed. Collector Books, 1998.

—. *Standard Encyclopedia of Opalescent Glass*. Collector Books, 1999.

Fauster, Carl. *Libbey Glass since 1818: Pictorial History and Collector's Guide.* Len Beach Press, 1979.

Feller, John Q. *Dorflinger: America's Finest Glass, 1852–1921*. Antique Publications, 1988.

Florence, Gene. *Elegant Glassware of the Depression Era,* 8th ed. Collector Books, 1999.

—. *Collector's Encyclopedia of Depression Glass,* 14th ed. Collector Books, 1998.

Heacock, William. *Encyclopedia of Victorian Colored Pattern Glass,* series vols. 1–9. Antique Publications, 1981–1998.

—. *Fenton Glass: The First Twenty-Five Years*. Antique Publications, 1978.

—. *Fenton Glass: The Second Twenty-Five Years*. Antique Publications, 1980.

—. *Fenton Glass: The Third Twenty-Five Years*. Antique Publications, 1989.

Husfloen, Kyle. *Collector's Guide to American Pressed Glass 1825–1915*. Wallace-Homestead, 1990.

Jenks, Bill, Jerry Luna, and Darryl Reilly. *Identifying Pattern Glass Reproductions.* Wallace-Homestead, 1993.

Jokelson, Paul, and Dena Tarshis. *Baccarat Paperweights and Related Glass 1820–1860.* Paperweight Press, 1990.

Lefkowith, Christie Mayer. *Art of Perfume: Discovering and Collecting Perfume Bottles.* Thames and Hudson, 1994.

Lindsey, Bessie M. *American Historical Glass.* Tuttle, 1967.

Long, Milbra, and Emily Seate. *Fostoria Stemware.* Collector Books, 1998.

—. *Fostoria Tableware, 1924–1943.* Collector Books, 1999.

—. *Fostoria Tableware, 1944–1986.* Collector Books, 2000.

—. *Fostoria Useful and Ornamental.* Collector Books, 2000.

McCain, Mollie H. *The Collector's Encyclopedia of Pattern Glass.* Collector Books, 1994.

McKearin, George S., and Helen McKearin. *American Glass.* Crown, 1948.

—. *Two Hundred Years of American Blown Glass.* Doubleday, 1950.

National Cambridge Collectors, Inc. *Colors in Cambridge Glass.* Collector Books, 1984.

Padgett, Leonard E. *Pairpoint Glass.* Wallace-Homestead, 1979

Perrot, Paul, Paul Gardner, and James S. Plaut. *Steuben: Seventy Years of American Glassmaking.* Praeger, 1974.

Pina, Leslie A. *Fostoria: Designer George Sakier: With Values.* Schiffer, 1996.

Revi, A. Christian. *American Cut and Engraved Glass.* Schiffer, 2000.

—. *Nineteenth Century Glass—Its Genesis and Development.* Schiffer, 1967.

Selman, Lawrence H. *All About Paperweights.* Paperweight Press, 1992.

Shuman, John A. III. *The Collector's Encyclopedia of American Art Glass.* Collector Books, 1987.

Sinclaire, Estelle F., and Jane Shadel Spillman. *The Complete Cut and Engraved Glass of Corning,* 2d ed. Syracuse University Press, 1997.

Spillman, Jane Shadel. *American and European Pressed Glass in the Corning Museum of Glass.* Corning Museum of Glass, 1981.

Weatherman, Hazel Marie. *Colored Glassware of the Depression Era,* book 2. Glassbooks, 1982.

—. *Fostoria: Its First 50 Years.* Glassbooks, 1972.

Weitman, Stan, and Arlene Weitman. *Crackle Glass: Identification and Value Guide,* vols. 1 and 2. Collector Books, 1996, 1998.

Wilson, Kenneth. *American Glass, 1760–1930: Toledo Museum of Art,* vols. 1 and 2. Hudson Hills Press, 1995.

——. *New England Glass and Glassmaking.* Crowell, 1972.

Art Glass

U.S. Art Glass
Arwas, Victor. *The Art of Glass: Art Nouveau to Art Deco.* Rizzoli International, 1997.

Cohen, Wilfred R. *Wave Crest: The Glass of C. F. Monroe.* Collector Books, 1987.

Dimitroff, Thomas P., Charles Hajdamach, and Jane Shadel Spillman. *Frederick Carder and Steuben Glass: American Classics.* Schiffer, 1998.

Duncan, Alastair. *Louis Comfort Tiffany.* Abrams, 1992.

Gardner, Paul V. *Frederick Carder: Portrait of a Glassmaker.* Crown, 1971.

Grover, Ray. *Art Glass Nouveau.* Tuttle, 1967.

——. *Carved and Decorated Art Glass.* Tuttle, 1971.

Koch, Robert. *Louis C. Tiffany: Rebel in Glass.* Crown, 1971.

McKean, Hugh F. *The (Lost) Treasures of Louis Comfort Tiffany.* Doubleday, 1980.

Meschi, Edward J. *Durand: The Man and His Glass.* Antique Publications, 1998.

Neustadt, Egon. *The Lamps of Tiffany.* Neustadt Museum of Tiffany Art, 1970.

Revi, Albert Christian. *American Art Nouveau Glass,* rev. ed. Thomas Nelson & Sons, 1967.

——. *Nineteenth Century Glass.* Thomas Nelson & Sons, 1968. Reprint, Schiffer, 1981.

Spillman, Jane Shadel. *Glass: Volume 1, Tableware, Bowls, and Vases.* Knopf, Chanticleer Press, 1986.

Steeg, Moise S. *Tiffany Favrile Art Glass.* Schiffer, 1997.

European Art Glass
Bacri, Clotilde. *Daum. Masters of French Decorative Glass.* Rizzoli, 1993.

Barovier, Marina. *Art of the Barovier, 1866–1972: Glassmakers in Murano.* Antique Collectors' Club, 1993.

Barr, Sheldon. *Venetian Glass: Confections in Glass 1855–1914.* Abrams, 1998.

Bayer, Patricia, and Mark Waller. *The Art of René Lalique.* Book Sales, 1988.

Bloch-Dermant, Janine. *The Art of French Glass.* Thames and Hudson, 1980.

Blount, Berniece, and Henry Blount. *French Cameo Glass.* Wallace-Homestead, 1968.

Dawes, Nicholas. *Lalique Glass.* Crown, 1986.

Garner, Phillipe, *The Art of Emile Gallé.* Rizzoli, 1979.

Grover, Lee, and Ray Grover. *English Cameo Glass.* Crown, 1980.

Grover, Ray, and Lee Grover. *Carved and Decorated European Glass.* Charles E. Tuttle
Co., 1970

Hajdamach, Charles. *British Glass, 1800–1914.* Antique Collectors' Club, 1991.

Heiremans, Marc. *Art Glass from Murano, 1910–1970.* Antique Collectors' Club,
1993.

——. *20th Century Murano Glass: From Craft to Design.* Arnoldsche Art Publishers,
1997.

Jackson, Leslie, ed. *Whitefriars Glass: The Art of James Powell & Sons.* Richard Dennis,
1996.

Neuwirth, Waltraud. *Glas Verre Vetri. I: 1950–60.* Austrian Museum of Fine Arts,,
1987.

Newman, Harold. *An Illustrated Dictionary of Glass.* Thames & Hudson, 1977.

Opie, Jennifer. *Scandinavia: Ceramics and Glass in the Twentieth Century.* Rizzoli, 1990.

Petrova, Sylva, and Jean-Luc Olivie, eds. *Bohemian Glass: 1400–1989.* Abrams, 1990.

Pina, Leslie A. *Fifties Glass.* Schiffer, 1993.

Ricke, Helmut, and Lars Thor, eds. *Swedish Glass Factories Production Catalogues,
1915–1960.* Prestel, 1987.

Tait, Hugh. *Glass 5,000 Years.* Abrams, 1991.

Truitt, Deborah, and Robert Truitt. *Bohemian Glass, 1880–1940,* vols. 1 and 2. B & D
Glass, 1995.

Whitehouse, Dr. David. *English Cameo Glass in the Corning Museum of Glass.* Corning
Museum of Glass, 1994.

Wickman, Kerstin, ed. *Orrefors, a Century of Swedish Glassmaking.* University of
Washington, 1999.

Studio Glass

Corning Museum Staff. *New Glass: A Worldwide Survey.* Corning Museum of Glass, 1981.

Fike, Bonita. *A Passion for Glass: The Aviva and Jack A. Robinson Studio Glass Collection.* Detroit Institute of Arts, 1998.

Frantz, Susanne K. *Contemporary Glass: A World Survey from the Corning Museum of Glass.* Corning Museum of Glass, 1989.

Grover, Ray, and Lee Grover. *Contemporary Art Glass.* Crown, 1975.

Klein, Dan. *Glass, a Contemporary Art.* Rizzoli International, 1989.

Miller, Bonnie J. *Out of the Fire: Contemporary Glass Artists and Their Work.* Chronicle Books, 1991.

Directories and Price Guides

Huxford, Sharon, and Bob Huxford, eds. *Schroeder's Antiques Price Guide,* 18th ed. Collector Books, 1999.

Maloney, David J. *Maloney's Antiques and Collectibles Resource Directory,* 5th ed. Antique Trader Books, 1999.
   Dealers, collectors, auctions, shows, repair and restoration experts, clubs, publications—includes anything and everything collectors need.

Schroy, Ellen T., ed. *Warman's Depression Glass: A Value and Identification Guide.* Chilton, 1997.

—. *Warman's Glass,* 3d ed. Krause, 1999.

—. *Warman's Pattern Glass.* Warman, 1993.

Agata: New England Peach Blow glass (see definition below) that has been further coated with a colored metallic stain, spattered with a volatile liquid leaving a glossy mottled surface, and then fired on. It was not signed.

Amberina: A transparent, single-layer glass shading from red to amber. It was originally made by the New England glass company and the Mt. Washington Glass Company. It was not signed. *The shaded glass types described in this glossary were all made by reheating part of the glass.*

Aurene: The name Frederic Carder gave to some of his Steuben iridescent glass, usually blue or gold.

Burmese: An opaque, single-layer glass shading from salmon-pink to yellow, sometimes enameled with flowers or animals. It was originally made by Mt. Washington and Thomas Webb. It was reproduced in the twentieth century by Gunderson-Pairpoint, Bryden-Pairpoint, and Fenton. Poor copies were exported from Murano.

Cameo glass: Two or more layers of glass, of contrasting colors, cut back in various ways to reveal a design. Other names for this technique are *overlay* and *acid cut-back.*

Crown Milano: A single-layer, opaque-white glass decorated with enameled motifs. It is sometimes signed CM. A similar line was named *Albertine.* Sometimes signed.

Depression glass: U.S. mass-produced glass made by many companies between 1920 and 1940. It was pressed in numerous patterns and made in a variety of colors. Some pieces are marked with a company logo.

Elegant glass: High quality, mass-produced tableware and stemware made by numerous U.S. companies from the late nineteenth century through the first half of the twentieth century.

Favrile: The name Tiffany gave to some of his iridescent blown or molded glass, usually gold or blue. It's usually signed. Favrile means *handmade.*

Filagrana: A Venetian technique in which opaque-white or colored threads of glass are laid out in a twisted or lace pattern and embedded in semi-hot glass and then reheated so that the glass threads are inside the finished glass.

Graal: A 1917 invention of Orrefors Company, Sweden. Layers of glass are cut back to reveal a pattern and then enclosed in a clear outer layer of glass. It is similar to what Steuben called Intarsia. The word *graal* is always in the signature.

Iridescent glass: Metallic vapors and oxides are sprayed onto the surface of still-hot glass, barely etching it but causing the surface to refract the light, creating a pearlescent effect of many hues.

Matte finish: A dull finish made by dipping a piece in an acid batch.

Millefiori (a thousand flowers): A Venetian decorating technique in which cross-sections of colored canes are embedded in clear molten glass in stylized floral patterns.

Mount Washington Lava: An opaque black glass with irregular pieces of different brightly colored glass embedded in the surface.

Mount Washington Peach Blow: An opaque single-layer glass shading from mauve pink to pale blue. It is not signed.

Mount Washington Napoli: A clear glass with externally raised, gold weblike partitions further decorated with colored enameled flowers or "Brownie" children. It is signed *Napoli.*

New England Peach Blow: An opaque single-layer glass shading form raspberry to creamy white. Never signed.

Opal glass: A translucent white glass.

Opaque glass: Glass that can't be seen through.

Plated Amberina: A New England Glass Company technique in which a red-to-yellow shaded glass was lined with a thin opal layer with vertical opal ribs. It is not signed.

Rock crystal glass: Deeply cut, engraved, and polished clear glass imitating Chinese quartz rock crystal. The designs were often Art Nouveau in style. This technique was popular in England and the U.S. from the 1880s to 1910. It is often signed either by the company or by the artist.

Royal Flemish: Single-layer, acid-finished glass with raised gold partitions that produce a stained-glass window effect. The glass is further decorated with colored stains, and enameled and gilded motifs. It is sometimes signed *RF.*

Staining: A technique in which the surface of cold glass is brushed with colored pigments that cover only designated parts of the glass, permeating the surface and leaving it smooth, not raised.

Sulphide paperweight: A paperweight in which a small, opaque-white medallion, made of a ceramic and/or glassy composite and molded into a portrait or other motif, is inserted into a semi-molten clear or single-colored glass and fired.

Tiffany aquamarine: Heavy, thick bowls or paperweights, pale blue-green, internally decorated with sea plants and marine life. These are very rare and are signed.

Tiffany lava: Glass in which basalt was added to the batch, creating a rough surface. Lava has a gold iridescence and may have coils of glass dripping down, looking like volcanic lava. It is signed.

Translucent: Semi-transparent glass.

Wheeling Peach Blow: A shaded glass, red to yellow, lined in white, made by the Hobbs Brockunier Company.

ABOUT THE INTERNATIONAL SOCIETY OF APPRAISERS

The *Collector's Compass* series is endorsed by the International Society of Appraisers, one of North America's leading nonprofit associations of professionally educated and certified personal property appraisers. Members of the ISA include many of the industry's most respected independent appraisers, auctioneers, and dealers.

ISA appraisers specialize in more than 200 areas of expertise in four main specialty pathways: antiques and residential contents, fine art, gems and jewelry, and machinery and equipment.

Established in 1979 and consisting of more than 1,375 members, the ISA is founded on two core principles: educating its members through a wide range of continuing education and training opportunities, and promoting and maintaining the highest ethical and professional standards in the field of appraisals.

Education through the ISA

In conjunction with the University of Maryland University College, the ISA offers a series of post-secondary professional courses in appraisal studies, including a two-level certification program.

The ISA recognizes three membership levels within its organization—Associate Member, Accredited Member, and Certified Member—with educational programs in place for achieving higher distinctions within the society. ISA members who complete the required course work are recognized with the title of Certified Appraiser of Personal Property (CAPP). Through its pioneering education programs, the ISA plays a vital role in producing qualified appraisers in appraisal theory, principles, procedures, ethics, and law as it pertains to personal property appraisal.

Professional Standards of the ISA

The ISA is dedicated to the highest ethical standards of conduct, ensuring public confidence in the ability and qualifications of its members. To help members perform their work with the most up-to-date knowledge of professional standards, the ISA is continually updating, expanding, and improving its courses and criteria of conduct.

For more information about the International Society of Appraisers, contact their corporate offices at:

Toll-free: 1-800-472-4732

E-mail: ISAHQ@isa-appraisers.org

Web site: www.isa-appraisers.org

ABOUT THE CONTRIBUTORS

Dianne Gregg received a BA from the American University, Washington, D.C. She became interested in art glass in 1972 when she studied glass with collector-teacher Ruth Suppes in Chevy Chase, Maryland, and was an instant devotee. Mrs. Gregg belongs to the National American Glass Club, where she was a director from 1989–1996. She's lectured to glass clubs on various subjects, teaches history and identification of European art glass, and has written articles for the *Glass Collectors' Digest*, the *Glass Club Bulletin*, the Journal of the National American Glass Club, and the *Acorn*, the Journal of the Sandwich Glass Museum. She became an accredited member of the International Society of Appraisers in 1993, and for several years has been a volunteer at the Ceramics and Glass Office at the Museum of American History of the Smithsonian Institution.

In 1989 her Chapter of the NAGC established the Blackistone Glass Periodical Study Center, of which she is the curator. The study center is at the Potomac Library, a Montgomery County, Maryland, public library. A public/private project that has been funded by the Glass Clubs, the center has an excellent primary-source collection of glass reference material.

Donald Tinney is a collector/dealer of American-made elegant glassware. He began collecting glass more than thirty-five years ago and became a dealer in 1983 when be started upgrading his collection. Along with his wife, Nedra Tinney, he formed NEDDON Antiques and has been buying and selling elegant glassware ever since.

Mr. Tinney's interest in various glass companies sparked his desire to learn more about them, so he became associated with the National Cambridge Collectors, Inc.; Fostoria Glass Society of America; and other national glass collectors' groups. He has served on the national board of directors of the Fostoria Glass Society of America, serving as vice president from 1999–2000. He is past president and a charter member of the Fostoria Glass Society of North Texas and was a founding member of Glass Plus Study Club in the Dallas area. He continues to educate himself on the history of various glass companies and their products by giving numerous programs on glass-related subjects for clubs and organizations.

Christopher J. Kuppig has spent his entire career in book publishing. For several years he directed programs at Dell Publishing, Consumer Reports Books, and most recently Chilton Book Company—where his assignments included managing the Wallace-Homestead and Warman's lines of antiques and collectibles guides.

In 1997, Mr. Kuppig founded Stone Studio Publishing Services, a general management consultancy to book publishers. Acting as Series Editor for the Collector's Compass series has given him the opportunity to draw upon his wide-ranging network of contacts in the collecting field.

Mr. Kuppig resides with his wife and three children in eastern Massachusetts.

INDEX

Numbers in italics indicate photos.

Amberina, 7, *26,* 26–27
Anchor Hocking, 13, *60*
antiques malls, 69–71, 117–18
appraisals, 99–101
Art Deco, 11–12, 22, 29, 37, 73
Art Nouveau, 10, 22, 28–29, 31–32, 35
auctions, 15–16, 44, 127–29
  Internet, 74–77
  live, 77–78, 115–16
Barovier, 39–40, *51, 52,* 94
Bohemian art glass, 35–36, 93, 94
books, 44, 135–39
British glass, 28, 94
Cambridge, *18,* 20, 30, *60–61*
  history, 36–37
  patterns, 13, 65
cameo glass, 28, 85
Carder, Frederick, 10, 37, 70
Carnival glass, 14–15, 18, 68, 85
Chihuly, Dale, 12, 40–41, *62–63*
cleaning, 108–109
collectors' clubs, 19–20, 46, 130–31
condition, 85–90
Corning, 25, 37
Dalzell–Viking, 65, 96
damage, 21, 87–88
dating, 91–92
Daum brothers, 11, 12, 29, 33, *49,* 94
dealers, 15, 47, 68, 69, 72–74, 78–81, 97–98
  acting as, 119–22
  selling to, 114
defects, 86
Depression glass, 13–15, *60–61,* 65, 73, *82,* 83
designers, 10–13, 37–41, 94
display, 47, 103–108

Durand, 10, *17,* 17, 94, *102,* 103
fakes, 15, 29, 93, 95–97
  at flea markets, 66–67
  at malls, 70
Favrile glass, 10, 22, 31
Fenton Glass Company, 18, *58, 59,* 65, *72,* 97
Fostoria, *18, 30, 59*
  history, 13, 30
  patterns, 90, 92
  reproductions, 96
French glass, 28–29, 94
Gallé, Emile, 10, 28–29, *50, 51,* 93, 94
galleries, 71, 126–27
Hald, Edward, 11, *33,* 33, 94
Hawkes, Thomas H.G., 37, 70
Heisey, *20,* 20, 30, 32, 58, 65, 73
  history, 13, 32
  museum, 20
history, 23–41
Hobbs, Brockunier, 7, 13, 25
Iittala, 12, *48,* 48, *54*
Imperial, 13, *20, 32,* 32, 37
insurance, 98, 99, 101, 106
Internet sales, 15–16, 74–77, 97, 118–19
Kosta, 12, 33–34, *56*
labels, 89–90
Labino, Domenic, 12, 40, 47, *63*
Lalique, 8, 11, 16–17, 85, 93, 94
Lalique, René, 10, 29, 52
Libbey Glass Company, 25–26, 93, 94
Lindstrand, Vicke, *34, 56,* 94
Littleton, Harvey, 12, 40, 47
Loetz, 7, 11, 35–36, 94
Lütken, Per, 48, *54, 55*
manufacturers, 10–13, 23–41, 94
Moser, Ludwig and Söhne, 35–36, *50,* 94
Mt. Washington Company, 7, 27, 93
Murano, 12, 38–39, 47, 94

museums, 20, 22, 131–34
New England Glass Company, 7, *26,* 26, 93
Nygren, John Fergus, 47, *62, 64*
Orrefors Glassworks, *11,* 11, 12, *33,* 33–34
packaging, 89–90
Peiser, Mark C., 47, *64*
price guides, 139
provenance, 95
publications, 19–20, 44, 116–17, 129
Quezel, *10,* 10, *15,* 94
rarity, 92
receipts, 72, 81, 97–98
record keeping, 97–99, 121–22
repairs, 88–89, 110–111
reproductions, 15, 95–97
Ritter, Richard Q. Jr, *64*
Scandinavian glass, 33–34, 94
selling, 113–22
shows, 15–16, 72–74, 120–21, 125–26
signatures, 47–48, 93
Steuben, *6,* 7, 11, *38, 53,* 57, 70, 85
  history, 10, 12, 33, 37
Stevens and Williams, 28, *42, 70,* 94
storage, 109–110
studio glass, 12, 47–48, 93
Thomas Webb Company, 27, 28, 94
Tiffany, 7, *8,* 8, *9,* 22, 31, 37, 85, 93
  Chihuly and, 40–41
  history, 31–32
  Loetz and, 35
Tiffany, Louis Comfort, 8, 10, 31, *53*
tools, 83–84
U.S. Glass, 13, 23, 25
value, 20–22, 84–95
Venini, Paolo, 12, 39, 40, *54,* 55, 94
Victorian glass, 9–10, 21–22, 85
Wirkkala, Tapio, 39, 65, 94